Jóhanna Sigurðardóttir

The First Openly Gay Prime Minister – Unauthorized

Rina Oliveira

ISBN: 9781779696830
Imprint: Telephasic Workshop
Copyright © 2024 Rina Oliveira.
All Rights Reserved.

Contents

Activism and Advocacy   16

Chapter 2: The Political Journey   31
Chapter 2: The Political Journey   31
A Desire for Political Change   34
Advocating for LGBTQ Rights in Politics   45

Chapter 3: A Prime Minister is Born   55
Chapter 3: A Prime Minister is Born   55
Political Turmoil and Leadership Crisis   57
Leading through Crisis   65

Chapter 4: Transforming Society   77
Chapter 4: Transforming Society   77
Legislative Victories for LGBTQ Rights   80
Inspiring Social Change   89

Chapter 5: Managing Personal and Public Life   97
Chapter 5: Managing Personal and Public Life   97
Navigating Relationships and Privacy   99
Challenges and Criticisms   105

Chapter 6: Legacy and Impact   111
Chapter 6: Legacy and Impact   111
Jóhanna's Lasting Influence   113

Index   123

1.1 Discovering Identity and Overcoming Obstacles

In this section, we will explore Jóhanna Sigurðardóttir's journey of self-discovery and the obstacles she faced along the way. From her early struggles with self-acceptance to navigating societal expectations and confronting discrimination, Jóhanna's story is one of resilience, determination, and the power of embracing one's true identity.

Early struggles with self-acceptance

Jóhanna Sigurðardóttir grew up in a small town in Iceland, where societal norms and expectations were deeply ingrained. From a young age, she felt different from her peers and struggled to understand her own feelings and emotions. As she began to discover her sexual orientation, she faced a whirlwind of confusion and fear.

Like many LGBTQ individuals, Jóhanna experienced a sense of isolation and internalized shame. She grappled with the societal stigma surrounding homosexuality, questioning her place in the world and whether she would ever find acceptance.

Example: One particular experience stands out in Jóhanna's memory. At the age of sixteen, she mustered the courage to confide in a close friend about her attraction to the same sex. Instead of support and understanding, she was met with ridicule and rejection. This incident left a lasting impact, deepening her struggle with self-acceptance.

Embracing her true identity

Despite the challenges she faced, Jóhanna eventually found the strength within herself to embrace her true identity. She embarked on a journey of self-discovery, seeking acceptance and happiness on her own terms.

Through self-reflection and personal growth, Jóhanna began to dismantle the internalized homophobia that had held her back for so many years. She surrounded herself with supportive and accepting friends, who helped her realize that her sexual orientation did not define her worth as a person.

Example: During her time in university, Jóhanna became involved with LGBTQ support groups and organizations. Committed to creating a safe and inclusive environment for others, she channeled her energy into activism and advocacy, fighting for LGBTQ rights and visibility.

Navigating societal expectations

As Jóhanna navigated her personal journey of self-acceptance, she also had to contend with the weight of societal expectations. Iceland was not yet the progressive nation it would become, and LGBTQ individuals faced discrimination and prejudice on a daily basis.

Jóhanna often found herself torn between the desire to live authentically and the pressure to conform to societal norms. She questioned whether she would ever be able to fully express her true self without facing judgment and backlash.

Example: In her late twenties, Jóhanna faced a pivotal moment in her life. She had to make a choice between living a closeted life, protecting herself from potential discrimination, or embracing her true identity and risking the consequences. She chose the latter, determined to overcome societal expectations and prove that LGBTQ individuals deserved respect and equal treatment.

Family support and acceptance

Throughout her journey, Jóhanna was fortunate to have the support and acceptance of her family. While societal attitudes towards homosexuality were still evolving, her loved ones provided a safe haven where she could be her authentic self.

Jóhanna's parents played a crucial role in her self-acceptance and empowerment. They embraced her sexual orientation with warmth and understanding, reinforcing the idea that her identity was something to be celebrated rather than hidden.

Example: When Jóhanna came out to her mother, she was met with open arms and words of love. Her mother's unwavering support gave her the courage to face the world with confidence and resilience, knowing that she had a foundation of love and acceptance to rely on.

Confronting discrimination and prejudice

As Jóhanna became more involved in activism and advocacy, she confronted discrimination and prejudice head-on. She refused to back down in the face of adversity, dedicating herself to creating a more inclusive and equal society for LGBTQ individuals.

Jóhanna's experiences with discrimination fueled her passion for change. She understood that her personal journey was not unique and that countless others faced similar struggles. This realization served as a driving force in her quest for justice and equality.

Example: Jóhanna encountered various forms of discrimination throughout her career. From being denied opportunities because of her sexual orientation to facing hateful rhetoric and insults, she persevered with unwavering determination. Each hurdle she faced only fueled her commitment to fighting for LGBTQ rights.

Turning adversity into motivation

Jóhanna's journey of discovering her identity and overcoming obstacles taught her the importance of resilience and determination. She refused to let adversity define her, instead transforming it into the fuel that propelled her forward.

By using her experiences as a catalyst for change, Jóhanna turned her personal struggles into a powerful motivation to fight for LGBTQ rights. She became a voice for the voiceless, advocating for equality, understanding, and acceptance.

Example: Jóhanna's resolve was put to the test when faced with backlash and resistance from those opposed to the LGBTQ movement. Instead of shying away from the opposition, she used it as an opportunity to educate and engage in meaningful dialogue. Through open discussions and sharing personal experiences, she sought to bridge the divide and build bridges of understanding.

In the next chapter, we will delve into Jóhanna's political journey, exploring how she channeled her passion for change into a career in politics and became a powerful advocate for LGBTQ rights within the political sphere.

1.1 Discovering Identity and Overcoming Obstacles

In this chapter, we explore the remarkable journey of Jóhanna Sigurðardóttir, the first openly gay Prime Minister. Jóhanna's path to self-discovery and acceptance was not without its challenges. From her early struggles with self-acceptance to navigating societal expectations and confronting discrimination, she overcame numerous obstacles to become a voice for change and pave the way for LGBTQ rights.

1.1.1 Early struggles with self-acceptance

Like many individuals in the LGBTQ community, Jóhanna faced an internal struggle in her early years. Growing up in a society where being gay was considered taboo, she grappled with understanding her own identity. She questioned herself, wondering if she could live authentically and openly in a world that often rejected people like her.

1.1.2 Embracing her true identity

Despite the challenges, Jóhanna eventually found the courage to embrace her true identity. She realized that denying who she was would only cause internal conflict and prevent her from living a fulfilling life. Accepting herself became the first step towards pursuing her dreams and advocating for change.

1.1.3 Navigating societal expectations

Coming to terms with her sexuality was one thing, but navigating societal expectations was an entirely different challenge. Jóhanna had to confront and question the norms and expectations placed upon her by society. She realized that by conforming to these expectations, she would be denying her true self. It was a difficult journey, but Jóhanna knew that true happiness would only come from living authentically.

1.1.4 Family support and acceptance

Throughout her journey, Jóhanna was fortunate to have the support and acceptance of her family. They stood by her side and encouraged her to be true to herself, despite any societal pressures or prejudices. Their unwavering love and understanding provided Jóhanna with the strength to overcome obstacles and pursue her dreams.

1.1.5 Confronting discrimination and prejudice

Jóhanna's path to self-acceptance was not smooth sailing. She faced discrimination and prejudice, both subtle and overt, from various aspects of society. However, instead of being deterred or silenced, Jóhanna chose to confront these challenges head-on. She became determined to fight against discrimination and prejudice, not only for herself but for the entire LGBTQ community.

1.1.6 Turning adversity into motivation

Adversity has a way of shaping individuals and providing them with the motivation to initiate change. Jóhanna had experienced enough discrimination and prejudice to fuel her passion for activism. She channeled her energy into advocacy and became an active participant in the LGBTQ rights movement. Jóhanna's personal experiences served as a driving force behind her dedication to creating a more inclusive and equal society.

Through her struggles with self-acceptance, navigating societal expectations, overcoming discrimination, and turning adversity into motivation, Jóhanna Sigurðardóttir embarked on a remarkable journey of discovering her identity and becoming a powerful advocate for LGBTQ rights. Her story serves as an inspiration to countless individuals, reminding us of the importance of embracing our true selves and fighting for the rights of all.

ERROR. thisXsection() returned an empty string with textbook depth = 3.
ERROR. thisXsection() returned an empty string with textbook depth = 3.
ERROR. thisXsection() returned an empty string with textbook depth = 3.

Embracing her true identity

Jóhanna Sigurðardóttir's journey of embracing her true identity was a transformative and empowering process. Like many LGBTQ individuals, she faced numerous challenges and struggles along the way. However, she was able to overcome these obstacles and find the strength to embrace her authentic self. This section will explore the key moments and experiences that shaped Jóhanna's journey of self-discovery and self-acceptance.

Early struggles with self-acceptance

Growing up in a society that often stigmatized and marginalized LGBTQ individuals, Jóhanna faced significant challenges when it came to accepting her own identity. In her early years, she struggled with feelings of confusion, fear, and shame. The societal pressure to conform to heterosexual norms made it difficult for her to understand and accept her sexual orientation.

Jóhanna's experiences of internalized homophobia were not uncommon. Many LGBTQ individuals go through a period of self-doubt and struggle to accept themselves due to the negative messages and attitudes prevalent in society. It took immense courage and self-reflection for Jóhanna to confront these internalized biases and embrace her true identity.

Embracing her true identity

Over time, Jóhanna began to question the expectations and norms imposed on her by society. She embarked on a journey of self-discovery, seeking to understand and acknowledge her true identity. This process included exploring her own feelings, thoughts, and desires, and accepting herself for who she truly was.

Embracing her true identity was not a smooth or linear process for Jóhanna. She faced moments of doubt, insecurity, and emotional upheaval. However, through self-reflection and self-compassion, she was able to gradually embrace her sexuality and come to terms with her authentic self.

Navigating societal expectations

As Jóhanna became more self-aware and accepting of her identity, she had to navigate societal expectations and norms that often invalidated her experiences. The pressure to conform to heterosexual expectations can be overwhelming for LGBTQ individuals, causing them to hide their true selves and deny their own happiness.

Jóhanna's journey of embracing her identity involved breaking free from these societal expectations and forging her own path. She had to find the courage to challenge traditional norms and live authentically, despite the potential backlash and judgment from others.

Family support and acceptance

Finding support from loved ones and family members can be crucial for LGBTQ individuals on their journey of self-acceptance. In Jóhanna's case, she was fortunate to have a supportive family who stood by her side throughout her journey.

Jóhanna's family played a pivotal role in helping her embrace her true identity. Their unconditional love and acceptance created a safe space for her to be her authentic self. Their support gave her the strength and confidence to fully embrace her sexuality and face the challenges that lay ahead.

Confronting discrimination and prejudice

Embracing her true identity also meant confronting the discrimination and prejudice that exist in society. LGBTQ individuals often face discrimination based on their sexual orientation or gender identity, which can take a toll on their self-esteem and mental well-being.

Jóhanna was no stranger to discrimination and prejudice. She encountered various forms of homophobia throughout her life, ranging from hurtful comments to overt acts of discrimination. However, rather than letting these experiences deter her, Jóhanna used them as fuel to fight for equality and justice.

Turning adversity into motivation

Throughout her journey of embracing her true identity, Jóhanna developed a resilience and determination that would shape her future activism. Instead of allowing the adversity she faced to hold her back, she used it as motivation to create a more inclusive society.

Jóhanna's ability to turn adversity into motivation is a testament to her strength and courage. Her personal experiences gave her a unique perspective on the challenges faced by LGBTQ individuals, which fueled her drive to advocate for change and fight for equal rights.

In conclusion, Jóhanna Sigurðardóttir's journey of embracing her true identity was a transformative and empowering process. From early struggles with self-acceptance to navigating societal expectations and confronting discrimination, Jóhanna's story serves as an inspiration for LGBTQ individuals around the world. Through her personal growth and activism, she has paved the way for a more accepting and inclusive society.

Navigating societal expectations

In this section, we will explore the challenges Jóhanna Sigurðardóttir faced in navigating societal expectations as she embraced her true identity as an LGBTQ individual. We will delve into the societal norms and pressures she encountered, as well as her strategies for overcoming them.

Societal norms and expectations

Growing up in Iceland during the mid-20th century, Jóhanna Sigurðardóttir found herself surrounded by societal norms that dictated strict gender roles and expectations. Traditional values and cultural norms made it difficult for individuals like Jóhanna to embrace and express their true identities. The prevailing belief was that marriage and family were defined solely as a union between a man and a woman.

These societal expectations often compelled LGBTQ individuals to conceal their true selves, leading to a sense of shame and fear of societal judgment. As Jóhanna grappled with her own identity, she was acutely aware of the immense pressure to conform to societal norms.

Challenging societal expectations

Despite the challenges she faced, Jóhanna Sigurðardóttir bravely decided to confront societal expectations head-on. She recognized that breaking free from societal constraints and embracing her true identity would not only be liberating for herself but would also pave the way for others like her.

Jóhanna devoted herself to challenging prevailing norms by advocating for LGBTQ rights and equality. She acknowledged that societal change could only happen if LGBTQ individuals and allies united forces to challenge discriminatory practices and educate society about the diverse spectrum of sexual orientations and gender identities.

Developing strategies for empowerment

To navigate societal expectations, Jóhanna developed several strategies to empower herself and others:

Education and awareness: Jóhanna understood that education was key to challenging societal expectations. She actively engaged in conversations and debates, sharing her personal experiences, and providing resources to dispel myths and misconceptions surrounding LGBTQ individuals.

Building alliances: Jóhanna realized the importance of building alliances with like-minded individuals and organizations. By collaborating with feminist groups, human rights activists, and LGBTQ organizations, she was able to create a support network that stood up against societal prejudices.

Visibility and representation: Jóhanna recognized the power of visibility and representation in changing societal perceptions. By openly embracing her identity, she inspired countless others to do the same. Her presence in the public eye offered hope and encouragement to those struggling with self-acceptance.

Leading by example: Jóhanna led by example, showing that LGBTQ individuals deserve the same rights, opportunities, and respect as anyone else. Through her activism and advocacy, she demonstrated that it was possible to thrive and make a positive impact despite societal pressures.

Real-life challenges and solutions

Jóhanna Sigurðardóttir faced numerous challenges in navigating societal expectations throughout her journey. Here, we highlight one such challenge and explore her innovative solution:

Challenge: Balancing personal and public life One of the greatest challenges Jóhanna faced was finding a balance between her personal and public life. As a trailblazing LGBTQ politician, her every move was scrutinized by the media and the public. This constant attention put a strain on her personal relationships and made it difficult for her to maintain boundaries.

Solution: Establishing personal boundaries and seeking support Jóhanna proactively tackled this challenge by establishing clear personal boundaries. She firmly communicated her need for privacy and emphasized the importance of separating her personal life from her political role.

Additionally, Jóhanna sought support from her trusted friends, family, and LGBTQ community. Their unwavering support provided her with the strength and resilience to navigate the complexities of her personal and public life.

The transformative power of navigating societal expectations

Jóhanna Sigurðardóttir's journey of navigating societal expectations serves as a powerful testament to the transformative impact of embracing one's true identity. By defying societal norms, she not only forged a path for herself but also sparked widespread change in Iceland and beyond.

Through her advocacy, she shattered stereotypes, challenged discriminatory practices, and championed LGBTQ rights. Her refusal to succumb to societal expectations and her commitment to authenticity inspired a generation of LGBTQ individuals to embrace their true selves, paving the way for greater acceptance and equality.

In the next chapter, we will explore Jóhanna's remarkable political journey, as she went on to become Iceland's first openly gay Prime Minister. This journey was vital in propelling LGBTQ rights to the forefront of the national agenda and further solidifying Jóhanna's legacy as a true champion of equality and social progress.

Family Support and Acceptance

Family support plays a crucial role in an individual's journey of self-acceptance, especially for someone like Jóhanna Sigurðardóttir, who faced early struggles with her own identity. In this section, we explore how Jóhanna's family provided the needed love, acceptance, and encouragement that allowed her to embrace her true self and navigate societal expectations.

Early Struggles with Self-Acceptance

As a young girl growing up in Iceland, Jóhanna encountered challenges in understanding and accepting her own identity. Like many LGBTQ individuals, she grappled with feelings of confusion and fear, unsure of how to reconcile her own experiences with societal norms. This internal struggle often leads to a sense of isolation and alienation.

Embracing her True Identity

Fortunately, Jóhanna found tremendous support from her family during her journey of self-discovery. Her parents, Ólafur and Sigurlína, provided a safe and nurturing environment where she felt the freedom to express herself authentically. Their unconditional love allowed Jóhanna to explore and understand her true identity without judgment or prejudice.

Navigating Societal Expectations

In a society that often imposed rigid expectations regarding gender and sexuality, Jóhanna relied on her family's support in navigating these societal norms. They encouraged her to embrace her uniqueness and defied societal pressures that sought to confine her to predefined roles. Their belief in her abilities allowed Jóhanna to challenge and redefine traditional norms.

Confronting Discrimination and Prejudice

While Jóhanna's family provided a loving and accepting environment, she still faced discrimination and prejudice from the broader community. Homophobia was prevalent, and LGBTQ individuals often faced social stigma and discrimination. Jóhanna's family, however, stood by her side, offering love, protection, and encouragement during these difficult times.

Turning Adversity into Motivation

Jóhanna's family taught her the value of resilience and turning adversity into motivation. Their unwavering support and belief in her abilities empowered her to rise above the challenges she encountered. By transforming negative experiences into fuel for change, Jóhanna became a powerful advocate for LGBTQ rights and an inspiration for countless others.

The Power of Acceptance

The importance of family support and acceptance cannot be overstated. For Jóhanna, her family played a pivotal role in her journey toward self-acceptance. Their continuous love, understanding, and encouragement gave her the strength to be true to herself, even in the face of societal adversity. Their support laid the groundwork for her future activism and leadership.

An Unconventional Example: The Power of Storytelling

One unconventional yet impactful practice that Jóhanna's family engaged in was the power of storytelling. Through the telling of personal experiences and narratives from the LGBTQ community, Jóhanna's parents created an environment of empathy, understanding, and awareness. By sharing stories of discrimination and triumph, they fostered an atmosphere of acceptance and educative conversations within their family.

Practical Steps for Families

For families seeking to support their LGBTQ members, here are some practical steps to consider:
    1. Open Communication: Encourage open dialogue to discuss feelings and experiences without judgment. 2. Unconditional Love: Embrace and accept your LGBTQ family member for who they are, no matter what. 3. Education and Awareness: Educate yourself and others about LGBTQ issues, discrimination, and legal rights. 4. Creating Safe Spaces: Ensure that home is a safe place where your LGBTQ family member can express themselves freely. 5. Advocacy: Stand up against discrimination and support LGBTQ organizations and causes. 6. Seek Professional Support: If needed, consider seeking guidance from LGBTQ support groups or therapists who specialize in LGBTQ issues.

Family support not only provides a foundation for LGBTQ individuals to navigate their personal challenges but also empowers them to make a difference in society. By embracing their LGBTQ family members, families can create a more inclusive and accepting world for all.

Confronting Discrimination and Prejudice

Throughout Jóhanna Sigurðardóttir's journey, she confronted countless instances of discrimination and prejudice due to her sexual orientation. This section explores the challenges she faced and the strategies she used to combat these societal barriers.

Early Struggles with Self-Acceptance

Jóhanna's journey towards self-acceptance was not an easy one. Growing up in a society that often stigmatized LGBTQ individuals, she experienced internal conflicts regarding her identity. The prevailing attitudes of the time made it challenging for her to embrace her true self and confront her own prejudices.

To overcome these struggles, Jóhanna embarked on a journey of self-discovery. She sought support from trusted friends, engaged in thoughtful introspection, and educated herself about LGBTQ issues. Through this process, she began to challenge the negative narratives society had imposed on her and cultivate a strong sense of self-acceptance.

Navigating Societal Expectations

As Jóhanna navigated her life and pursued her ambitions, she faced societal expectations that confined her within traditional gender roles. These expectations limited her opportunities for personal and professional growth and reinforced prejudices prevalent in Icelandic society.

Jóhanna defied these expectations by fearlessly confronting norms and refusing to be confined by societal limitations. She pursued her education, entered the workforce, and embarked on her political journey, all while challenging gender stereotypes. By breaking barriers and proving that gender has no bearing on one's abilities or potential, she shattered stereotypes and paved the way for future LGBTQ leaders.

Family Support and Acceptance

Jóhanna's journey was bolstered by the unwavering support and acceptance she received from her family. From the earliest stages of her career and activism, her loved ones stood by her side, providing a strong foundation of support and love. This support was instrumental in helping her confront discrimination and prejudice with resilience and determination.

By highlighting the importance of family acceptance, Jóhanna showcased the power of unconditional love in challenging societal prejudices. Her experience demonstrates that familial support can greatly impact an individual's ability to navigate discrimination, fostering an environment in which they can fully embrace their true selves.

Confronting Discrimination and Prejudice

Jóhanna confronted numerous instances of discrimination and prejudice throughout her life, both personally and professionally. Whether it was facing derogatory comments or being excluded from political circles due to her sexual orientation, she never backed down from defending her rights and the rights of the LGBTQ community.

She employed various strategies to dismantle discrimination and prejudice. Jóhanna used her platform as an activist and politician to raise awareness about LGBTQ issues, educate the public, and challenge harmful stereotypes. She tirelessly advocated for equal rights, fought against discriminatory legislation, and promoted inclusivity and diversity.

Furthermore, she built alliances and formed networks with like-minded individuals who shared her vision for a more tolerant society. By collaborating with allies within and outside of the LGBTQ community, Jóhanna amplified her voice and strengthened her impact, ensuring that her fight for equality reached a broader audience.

Turning Adversity into Motivation

Despite the discrimination she faced, Jóhanna never allowed herself to become disheartened. Instead, she used those experiences as fuel for her activism and as motivation to effect meaningful change. Jóhanna transformed the negativity she encountered into a driving force, propelling her towards creating a more inclusive society.

Through her courageous and resilient response to prejudice, Jóhanna empowered others to confront discrimination in their own lives. Her journey serves as an inspiration to those who face adversity, demonstrating that perseverance and determination can lead to impactful social change.

In summary, this section explores how Jóhanna Sigurðardóttir confronted discrimination and prejudice throughout her life. It highlights her early struggles with self-acceptance, the societal expectations she faced, the crucial role of family support, and her strategies for challenging discrimination. Jóhanna's resilience and determination serve as a beacon of hope for those fighting against prejudice and discrimination, encouraging individuals to embrace their true selves and advocate for a more inclusive world.

Turning adversity into motivation

In this section, we will delve into how Jóhanna Sigurðardóttir turned adversity into motivation, harnessing her struggles and challenges to drive her activism and advocacy work. This journey of transforming hardships into fuel for change is a testament to her resilience and determination.

Early struggles with self-acceptance

Jóhanna's journey toward self-acceptance was not always an easy one. Like many LGBTQ individuals, she grappled with societal expectations and the pressure to conform. Growing up in a conservative society, she faced significant challenges in embracing her true identity. At a time when being openly gay was far from accepted, Jóhanna had to confront her own fears and internalized homophobia.

Embracing her true identity

Despite the obstacles, Jóhanna eventually found the strength to embrace her true identity. She came to the realization that authenticity and self-acceptance were vital for personal happiness and fulfillment. Through self-reflection and inner growth, she embarked on a journey of self-discovery, gradually shedding the mask imposed by society and fully embracing her identity as a gay woman.

Navigating societal expectations

In a society where heteronormativity was the norm, Jóhanna had to navigate conflicting expectations. As a woman, there were societal pressures for her to conform to traditional gender roles and marry a man. However, she refused to let societal expectations define her. Instead, she chose to challenge those expectations and chart her path authentically, setting an inspiring example for others facing similar struggles.

Family support and acceptance

The support and acceptance of Jóhanna's family played an instrumental role in her journey. They stood by her side, providing a foundation of love and support during challenging times. This unwavering support gave her strength and propelled her forward, enabling her to channel her energy into making a difference in the lives of LGBTQ individuals.

Confronting discrimination and prejudice

Jóhanna's personal experiences with discrimination and prejudice only fueled her determination to fight for equality and justice. She faced adversity head-on, refusing to be silenced by those who sought to marginalize her. Her resilience in the face of discrimination not only strengthened her resolve but also inspired others to join the movement for LGBTQ rights.

Turning adversity into motivation

Rather than succumbing to despair or bitterness, Jóhanna turned her experiences of adversity into motivation. She recognized that her struggles were not unique and that countless others faced similar challenges. This empathy and understanding drove her to advocate not only for her own rights but also for the rights of the entire LGBTQ community.

Jóhanna harnessed her personal experiences to fuel her activism and create change. She used her platform to raise awareness about the discrimination faced by LGBTQ individuals, pushing for reforms and legislation that would safeguard their rights. Through her motivational speeches, she urged individuals to transform their own adversities into catalysts for positive change, inspiring a generation of activists to rise up and fight against discrimination in all its forms.

Example: Overcoming barriers in political activism

As an openly gay politician, Jóhanna faced numerous hurdles in her journey towards political activism. She encountered prejudice from fellow politicians, skepticism from the public, and significant opposition to her advocacy for LGBTQ rights. However, rather than being deterred by these barriers, Jóhanna channeled her adversity into motivation.

She transformed her early struggles with self-acceptance and societal expectations into a driving force for change within political circles. Instead of conforming to the status quo, she confronted discrimination and challenged traditional political norms. Her relentless efforts paid off, propelling her into positions of influence where she could effect real change.

Trick: The power of personal storytelling

One of the most powerful tools Jóhanna employed in turning adversity into motivation was the art of personal storytelling. By openly sharing her own struggles and triumphs, she humanized the LGBTQ rights movement and created a connection with individuals who may have previously been indifferent or opposed to gay rights.

Jóhanna's personal narrative of resilience and transformation served as a beacon of hope for those grappling with their own adversity. Through her storytelling, she reached hearts and minds, breaking down barriers and fostering empathy. By sharing our own stories, we too can inspire change and motivate others to fight for what is just and right.

Exercise: Reflecting on personal adversities

Take a moment to reflect on a personal adversity you have faced in your own life. Consider how that experience has shaped you and the lessons you have learned from it. Think about how you can use the motivation derived from that adversity to make a positive impact in your community or advocate for a cause you believe in. Write down your thoughts and commit to taking action.

Conclusion

Jóhanna Sigurðardóttir's ability to turn adversity into motivation serves as a powerful example for all of us. Her journey of self-acceptance, resilience, and unwavering advocacy for LGBTQ rights inspires us to confront our own challenges head-on and transform them into vehicles for change. By harnessing the power of personal storytelling and empathy, we can follow in Jóhanna's footsteps, creating a more inclusive and just society for all.

Activism and Advocacy

Organizing within the LGBTQ Community

Organizing within the LGBTQ community is a vital component of any activist movement. It is through this organization that individuals can come together, share experiences, and form a powerful collective voice for change. In this section, we will explore the various aspects of organizing within the LGBTQ community, including the importance of community support, effective communication strategies, and grassroots mobilization.

The Power of Community Support

One of the fundamental pillars of organizing within the LGBTQ community is the power of community support. LGBTQ individuals often face unique challenges and struggles, and finding a safe and inclusive space where they can share their experiences is essential. Community support provides a sense of belonging and validation, fostering resilience and empowering individuals to advocate for their rights.

In organizing within the LGBTQ community, support groups play a crucial role. These groups provide a platform for individuals to come together, seek guidance, and offer mutual support. From LGBTQ youth groups to support networks for transgender individuals, these groups create a sense of solidarity and empower marginalized voices.

Effective Communication Strategies

Effective communication is key to successful organizing within the LGBTQ community. Advocates must be able to convey their message clearly and engage with diverse audiences. In the digital age, utilizing various communication platforms is crucial in reaching a wider audience and fostering engagement.

Social media has revolutionized the way LGBTQ activists communicate and mobilize. Platforms such as Twitter, Facebook, and Instagram enable advocates to share stories, raise awareness, and organize events. Hashtags and viral campaigns have become powerful tools for spreading messages and creating online communities. For example, the hashtag #LoveIsLove has been used globally to support LGBTQ equality and challenge discriminatory laws.

In addition to online communication, grassroots organizing and face-to-face interactions remain important. Events such as Pride parades, rallies, and town hall meetings provide opportunities for LGBTQ activists to connect with their local community, build alliances, and generate support. These events allow for personal connections and meaningful conversations, fostering greater understanding and empathy.

Grassroots Mobilization

Grassroots mobilization is an integral part of organizing within the LGBTQ community. This approach focuses on empowering individuals at the local level and encouraging them to take action. By mobilizing grassroots support, activists can create a powerful force for change and challenge systemic inequalities.

To effectively mobilize within the LGBTQ community, organizers must engage in strategic planning, coalition-building, and grassroots advocacy. This involves identifying key issues, setting clear goals, and developing effective strategies to achieve them. Collaborating with other social justice movements and embracing intersectionality is critical in building a broad-based movement for equality, as the struggles for LGBTQ rights intersect with other forms of oppression.

Mobilization efforts can take various forms, such as community outreach, public demonstrations, and lobbying policymakers. By building relationships with elected officials, activists can influence policy decisions and promote legislative changes that protect LGBTQ individuals from discrimination and ensure equal rights.

An Unconventional Approach: Queer Spectacles

While traditional organizing methods such as meetings and campaigns are essential, there is room for unconventional approaches within the LGBTQ community. One such approach is the concept of "queer spectacles." Queer spectacles involve using creative, attention-grabbing events or performances to challenge norms and spark conversations.

For example, in 2012, LGBTQ activists staged a "kiss-in" protest at a Chick-fil-A restaurant after its CEO made anti-LGBTQ remarks. Couples gathered at the fast-food chain and engaged in public displays of affection to advocate for LGBTQ equality. This spectacle not only garnered media attention but also sparked dialogue and raised awareness about LGBTQ rights.

Queer spectacles provide a unique opportunity to reach a broader audience, challenge societal norms, and create memorable experiences that inspire change. These events can range from flash mobs to street art installations, effectively disrupting the status quo and promoting dialogue.

Key Takeaways

Organizing within the LGBTQ community requires the power of community support, effective communication strategies, grassroots mobilization, and at times, unconventional approaches like queer spectacles. By coming together, advocating for their rights, and challenging societal norms, LGBTQ activists can make a profound impact on their communities and beyond. Through organizing, the LGBTQ community can create lasting change, promote inclusivity, and pave the way for a more equitable society.

Fighting for Equality and Legal Protections

In this section, we delve into Jóhanna Sigurðardóttir's tireless efforts in fighting for equality and legal protections for the LGBTQ community. Jóhanna's activism went hand in hand with her political career, as she used her position to champion LGBTQ rights in Iceland and beyond.

Realizing the Need for Change

Jóhanna Sigurðardóttir, being a member of the LGBTQ community herself, understood firsthand the struggles and discrimination faced by individuals like her. She recognized the need for change and realized that the fight for equality and legal protections was essential for the wellbeing and happiness of LGBTQ individuals.

The Importance of Legislative Changes

One of the key aspects of Jóhanna's fight for LGBTQ rights was the push for legislative changes. She understood that laws played a significant role in shaping societal attitudes and protecting individuals from discrimination. Jóhanna worked tirelessly to introduce and pass laws that would safeguard the rights of LGBTQ individuals and grant them the same legal protections as their heterosexual counterparts.

Championing Same-Sex Marriage

One of the major battles fought by Jóhanna was the legalization of same-sex marriage. She recognized that marriage equality was not just about legal recognition but also about validation and acceptance. Jóhanna relentlessly advocated for the rights of same-sex couples to marry, challenging societal norms and deeply ingrained prejudices. Through her efforts, Iceland became one of the first countries in the world to legalize same-sex marriage in 2010.

Advocating Against Discrimination

Jóhanna Sigurðardóttir fought fervently to protect LGBTQ individuals from all forms of discrimination. She recognized that discrimination not only affected an individual's quality of life but also hindered their personal and professional growth. Jóhanna pushed for laws that would make it illegal to discriminate against individuals based on their sexual orientation or gender identity, ensuring equal opportunities for all.

International Influence

Jóhanna's fight for equality and legal protections had a significant impact both domestically and internationally. Her successes in Iceland became a shining example for other nations, inspiring movements and legislation changes worldwide. Jóhanna used her platform to advocate for LGBTQ rights on the global stage, fostering international dialogue and encouraging other countries to follow suit.

Collaboration and Unity

One of the defining aspects of Jóhanna's activism was her ability to collaborate and build alliances with like-minded politicians and activists. She understood that unity and collaboration were essential in bringing about meaningful change. Jóhanna worked closely with LGBTQ organizations and activists, as well as fellow politicians who shared her vision, to create a stronger and unified voice for equality.

Balancing Activism and Political Responsibilities

Throughout her political journey, Jóhanna Sigurðardóttir faced the challenge of balancing her activism with her political responsibilities. She had to navigate the delicate balance between pushing for change and fulfilling her duties as a politician in a broader sense. Jóhanna managed to find the middle ground, effectively using her position to advance LGBTQ rights while still advocating for a broader range of social and political issues.

In conclusion, Jóhanna Sigurðardóttir's fight for equality and legal protections for the LGBTQ community demonstrated her unwavering commitment to creating a more inclusive society. Through legislative victories, advocacy, collaboration, and international influence, Jóhanna left an indelible mark on Iceland and the world. Her legacy continues to inspire future LGBTQ leaders and shape attitudes towards LGBTQ individuals, paving the way for a more accepting and equitable world.

Becoming a voice for change

In the journey towards LGBTQ equality, Jóhanna Sigurðardóttir emerged as a powerful voice for change. Through her activism and advocacy, she played a pivotal role in fighting for LGBTQ rights and securing legal protections for the community. Her relentless determination and unwavering commitment to equality made her a beacon of hope for countless LGBTQ individuals around the world.

Organizing within the LGBTQ community

Jóhanna Sigurðardóttir recognized the importance of organizing within the LGBTQ community to bring about meaningful change. She actively participated in LGBTQ organizations and grassroots movements, working tirelessly to raise awareness and mobilize support for equal rights. By connecting with individuals who shared her vision, Jóhanna built a strong network of like-minded activists who were dedicated to advancing LGBTQ rights.

Fighting for equality and legal protections

Driven by a deep sense of justice, Jóhanna fought tirelessly for LGBTQ equality and legal protections. By becoming intimately familiar with the legal landscape, she strategically utilized her influence to challenge discriminatory laws and policies. Her relentless efforts led to significant legal victories, including the legalization of same-sex marriage, the protection of LGBTQ individuals from discrimination, and the recognition of adoption rights for same-sex couples.

Becoming a role model and inspiring others

Jóhanna's journey as an openly gay politician and activist made her a powerful role model, inspiring countless LGBTQ individuals to embrace their true selves and fight for their rights. Her courage in the face of adversity instilled hope and confidence in those who had been marginalized and silenced. By sharing her personal story, Jóhanna touched hearts and minds, encouraging others to stand up for equality and challenge societal norms.

Collaborating with like-minded politicians

Jóhanna understood the importance of collaboration in driving systemic change. She formed alliances with like-minded politicians who shared her commitment to LGBTQ rights. By working together, they were able to amplify their voices and build a stronger case for equality. Through strategic partnerships, Jóhanna and her colleagues were able to pass groundbreaking legislation that advanced LGBTQ rights and created a more inclusive society.

Balancing activism with political responsibilities

As an openly gay politician, Jóhanna faced the unique challenge of balancing her activism with her political responsibilities. She navigated this delicate balance with grace and resilience, ensuring that her advocacy work did not compromise her ability to effectively govern. Jóhanna's ability to bridge the gap between activism and politics allowed her to create meaningful change from within the system while continuing to advocate for LGBTQ rights.

Making a lasting impact

Jóhanna Sigurðardóttir's unwavering dedication to LGBTQ equality has left an indelible mark on society. Her instrumental role in advancing LGBTQ rights in Iceland and beyond has paved the way for future leaders and activists. By challenging societal norms, breaking down barriers, and championing the rights of marginalized communities, Jóhanna has transformed attitudes and perceptions of LGBTQ individuals, leaving a lasting legacy of inclusivity and acceptance.

Example Problem: One of the key legal victories that Jóhanna Sigurðardóttir achieved was the legalization of same-sex marriage. However, the fight for marriage equality was not without obstacles.

Problem: In a hypothetical country, same-sex marriage is not recognized, and there is significant opposition from conservative groups. LGBTQ activists are campaigning for the legalization of same-sex marriage, but they face significant resistance. How can they effectively advocate for marriage equality and overcome the opposition?

Solution:

To effectively advocate for marriage equality and overcome opposition, LGBTQ activists can employ several strategies:

1. Raise awareness: By educating the public about the importance of marriage equality and dispelling myths and misconceptions, activists can garner support for their cause. This can be done through public campaigns, media appearances, and community engagement.

2. Engage with religious groups: Addressing concerns from religious communities is crucial in challenging opposition to same-sex marriage. LGBTQ activists can initiate dialogue and foster understanding, emphasizing that marriage equality does not undermine religious freedom but rather promotes equality for all.

3. Mobilize support: Building a broad coalition of supporters is essential in countering opposition. Activists can collaborate with other progressive groups, human rights organizations, and influential allies to form a united front and demonstrate the widespread support for marriage equality.

4. Emphasize the human rights aspect: Frame the fight for marriage equality as a matter of fundamental human rights. Highlight the impact of discriminatory laws on LGBTQ individuals and their families, emphasizing the importance of equality, love, and dignity for all.

5. Lobby for legislative change: Activists can engage with lawmakers, urging them to introduce bills or support existing legislation that legalizes same-sex

marriage. By providing evidence and research on the positive impacts of marriage equality, activists can make a compelling case for legal recognition.

6. Harness the power of personal stories: Sharing personal stories of LGBTQ individuals and their experiences of love, commitment, and family can be a powerful tool in humanizing the fight for marriage equality. These stories can resonate with the general public, fostering empathy and understanding.

By employing these strategies, LGBTQ activists can effectively advocate for marriage equality and overcome opposition, ultimately creating a more inclusive and equal society.

Forming alliances and building a support network

Forming alliances and building a support network are essential steps in any successful activism movement. Jóhanna Sigurðardóttir's journey as an LGBTQ activist and politician was no exception. In this section, we will explore how Jóhanna formed alliances and built a support network, which played a crucial role in her advocacy and eventual appointment as Prime Minister of Iceland.

The Power of Collaboration

Collaboration is the key to creating change on a larger scale. Jóhanna understood this principle and actively sought partnerships with other activists, organizations, and politicians who shared her vision for equality. By joining forces with like-minded individuals and groups, Jóhanna was able to amplify her voice and expand her reach.

One way Jóhanna formed alliances was by participating in LGBTQ community events and connecting with fellow activists. Pride parades, rallies, and conferences provided a platform for Jóhanna to meet and collaborate with individuals who were fighting for LGBTQ rights. These events not only fostered a sense of solidarity but also allowed Jóhanna to share her experiences and learn from others' perspectives.

Building a Support Network

Building a strong support network was crucial for Jóhanna not only as an activist but also as a politician. She sought out mentors, advisors, and allies who could provide guidance and support in navigating the complex landscape of politics and policy-making. These relationships allowed Jóhanna to learn from experienced leaders and gain insights into effective strategies for creating change.

Jóhanna also relied on her personal connections to build her support network. Friends, family, and colleagues who believed in her cause became her pillars of strength. Their unwavering support and encouragement gave her the confidence to push forward, even in the face of adversity.

Alliances beyond LGBTQ Advocacy

While Jóhanna dedicated herself to LGBTQ advocacy, she recognized the importance of forming alliances with individuals and organizations from diverse backgrounds. She understood that social change requires collaboration across various issues and communities.

Jóhanna actively sought opportunities to collaborate with politicians and activists working on other progressive causes such as gender equality, environmental protection, and human rights. By connecting with these individuals, she was able to build bridges and cultivate support for LGBTQ rights within broader social justice movements.

Unconventional Tactics for Building Alliances

Jóhanna's commitment to LGBTQ rights extended beyond traditional alliances. She also sought unconventional ways to build support for her cause. For example, Jóhanna actively reached out to celebrities, influential figures, and public personalities who could use their platforms to raise awareness and promote LGBTQ equality. This approach helped her gain visibility and support from a wider audience.

Additionally, Jóhanna recognized the power of storytelling in creating empathy and understanding. She actively shared her personal journey and experiences as an LGBTQ individual, allowing others to connect with her on a deeper level. By sharing her story, she was able to humanize the LGBTQ rights movement and build bridges with individuals who may not have otherwise supported her cause.

Exercises: Building Your Support Network

1. Identify three organizations or individuals who are working towards a cause you are passionate about. Reach out to them and explore opportunities for collaboration or support.

2. Attend a community event or conference focused on social justice issues. Take the time to connect with like-minded individuals and consider how you can form alliances to further your advocacy work.

3. Reflect on your personal connections. Identify friends, family members, or colleagues who may be supportive of your cause. Talk to them about your passions and seek their input and guidance.

4. Think about unconventional ways to raise awareness for your cause. Consider reaching out to public figures or using storytelling as a means of connecting with others.

Remember, building a support network takes time and effort. Be patient, persistent, and open to new opportunities for collaboration. Together, we can create lasting change.

Gaining recognition and influence

In order for Jóhanna Sigurðardóttir to bring about real change as an LGBTQ activist, she needed to gain recognition and influence within her community and beyond. This section explores the strategies she employed to achieve this and the impact she made as a result.

Building a network of support

Jóhanna understood the power of forming alliances and building a support network. She actively sought out like-minded individuals who shared her passion for LGBTQ rights and worked collaboratively with them. By joining forces, they were able to amplify their voices and advocate for change more effectively.

To build her network, Jóhanna participated in LGBTQ organizations and attended conferences and events dedicated to promoting equality and inclusivity. This allowed her to connect with others who were equally invested in the cause and create a platform for sharing ideas, strategies, and resources. By surrounding herself with passionate individuals, Jóhanna gained recognition within the LGBTQ community as a trusted advocate and leader.

Using her platform for advocacy

As Jóhanna's voice gained prominence within the LGBTQ community, she understood the importance of using her platform for advocacy. She regularly spoke at public events, conferences, and rallies, passionately articulating the need for equality and legal protections. Her speeches were not only inspiring but also educational, as she effectively communicated the challenges faced by LGBTQ individuals and the detrimental impact of discrimination.

Jóhanna leveraged her position to raise awareness and gain visibility for LGBTQ issues. She engaged with the media, granting interviews and sharing her personal journey. By being open and vulnerable about her own struggles and triumphs, she humanized LGBTQ experiences and encouraged empathy and understanding from the wider public.

Collaborating with influential figures

Recognizing the power of collaboration, Jóhanna reached out to influential figures within politics, the arts, and the media. By working with individuals who had a strong platform and public support, she was able to amplify her messages and gain credibility.

She formed alliances with celebrities, artists, and activists who were passionate about LGBTQ rights. This collaboration not only increased her visibility but also helped to shift public perceptions by presenting LGBTQ issues in a relatable and non-threatening way. Through joint ventures and public appearances, Jóhanna was able to reach a wider audience and engage with people who may not have previously considered LGBTQ rights as a priority.

Overcoming obstacles and staying resilient

Throughout her journey, Jóhanna faced various obstacles and encountered resistance from those who opposed LGBTQ rights. However, she remained resilient and determined, using every setback as an opportunity to learn and grow.

She utilized her experiences of discrimination and prejudice to fuel her activism, turning adversity into motivation. This unwavering dedication further solidified her reputation as a passionate advocate for change, gaining her recognition not only within the LGBTQ community but also among allies and supporters.

Expanding influence on a national scale

As Jóhanna's influence grew, she began to make a significant impact on a national scale. Her tireless advocacy efforts contributed to shifting public opinion and paved the way for legislative changes. She worked closely with political allies to draft and introduce bills that protected LGBTQ individuals from discrimination and ensured their equal rights in various aspects of life.

By actively engaging with politicians, Jóhanna built relationships and gained their support for LGBTQ rights. Her ability to navigate the political landscape and work collaboratively resulted in the successful passage of crucial legislation for marriage equality, anti-discrimination measures, and adoption rights.

Empowering future generations

Jóhanna's influence extended beyond her own achievements, as she actively mentored and empowered future LGBTQ activists. She recognized the importance of cultivating the next generation of advocates and leaders. Through mentorship programs and educational initiatives, she encouraged young LGBTQ individuals to embrace their identities and be unapologetically themselves.

Jóhanna's legacy lives on through the individuals she inspired, who continue to fight for equality and advance LGBTQ rights. Her influence transcends national boundaries, inspiring activists around the world to be bold, visible, and unyielding in their pursuit of justice and inclusivity.

In conclusion, Jóhanna Sigurðardóttir gained recognition and influence as an LGBTQ activist through building a network of support, using her platform for advocacy, collaborating with influential figures, staying resilient in the face of obstacles, expanding her influence on a national scale, and empowering future generations. Her tireless efforts and unwavering commitment have left an indelible mark on the fight for LGBTQ rights, making her an iconic figure in the movement.

Making a difference on a national scale

Jóhanna Sigurðardóttir's impact on Iceland was not limited to her activism and advocacy within the LGBTQ community. As the country's first openly gay Prime Minister, she had the opportunity to make a difference on a national scale, implementing policies that transformed the society and paved the way for equality and acceptance. In this section, we will explore some of the key initiatives and legislative changes spearheaded by Jóhanna that left a lasting impact on Iceland.

1.3.6.1 Social equality and welfare reforms

One of Jóhanna's key focuses as Prime Minister was to promote social equality and welfare reforms, ensuring that all citizens, regardless of their gender, sexual orientation, or socioeconomic status, had access to essential services and resources. She recognized that true equality could not be achieved without addressing the systemic barriers that marginalized communities face.

To tackle this issue, Jóhanna implemented a series of policy changes aimed at reducing income inequality and improving social welfare. She introduced progressive taxation reforms to redistribute wealth more fairly, ensuring that the burden of taxation fell on those with higher incomes. Additionally, Jóhanna expanded the social support system, providing increased financial assistance to low-income families, single parents, and vulnerable populations.

Furthermore, Jóhanna advocated for gender equality by implementing legislation that mandated equal pay for equal work. She recognized the importance of closing the gender wage gap and ensuring that women had the same opportunities for career advancement and financial stability as men. These initiatives not only benefited the LGBTQ community but also improved the lives of all Icelanders, creating a fairer and more inclusive society.

1.3.6.2 Education and awareness programs

Jóhanna understood the importance of education and awareness in promoting LGBTQ acceptance and combating discrimination. She believed that change starts with the youth and that it was crucial to instill values of tolerance, respect, and equality from an early age.

To achieve this, Jóhanna introduced comprehensive sex education programs in schools that included LGBTQ-inclusive content. These programs provided students with accurate information about sexuality, gender identity, and relationships, promoting understanding and acceptance of diverse identities.

Additionally, Jóhanna supported the development of awareness campaigns and workshops that aimed to challenge stereotypes, debunk myths, and foster a safe and inclusive environment for LGBTQ individuals. These initiatives sparked conversations and dialogue, encouraging people to examine their own biases and prejudices.

1.3.6.3 Hate crime legislation and victim support

Jóhanna was a strong advocate for the protection of LGBTQ individuals from hate crimes and discrimination. She recognized the importance of implementing legislation that not only condemned such acts but also provided support to victims and held perpetrators accountable.

Under her leadership, hate crime legislation was strengthened, ensuring that LGBTQ individuals were protected under the law. The penalties for hate crimes based on sexual orientation or gender identity were harsher, sending a clear message that violence and discrimination would not be tolerated.

Furthermore, Jóhanna prioritized the establishment of victim support services specifically tailored to the needs of LGBTQ individuals. These services provided counseling, legal representation, and assistance in navigating the criminal justice system. By addressing the unique challenges faced by victims of hate crimes, Jóhanna aimed to create a safer and more inclusive society for all.

1.3.6.4 International advocacy and influence

Jóhanna's impact extended beyond Iceland's borders, as she used her position as Prime Minister to advocate for LGBTQ rights on the international stage. She

ACTIVISM AND ADVOCACY

sought to create alliances with like-minded politicians and activists from around the world, forming a global network dedicated to advancing equality and securing legal protections for LGBTQ individuals.

Through her involvement in international conferences and forums, Jóhanna raised awareness about the challenges faced by the LGBTQ community and urged other countries to adopt progressive policies. Her influence helped shape the global discourse on LGBTQ rights, inspiring other leaders to take action and creating momentum for change.

Additionally, Jóhanna's efforts to promote LGBTQ acceptance and inclusivity positioned Iceland as a global leader in the fight for equality. The country became known for its progressive policies and forward-thinking approach, attracting tourists and investors who valued diversity and social progress.

1.3.6.5 Cultural impact and media representation

As the first openly gay Prime Minister, Jóhanna became a symbol of hope and inspiration for LGBTQ individuals around the world. Her story resonated with people who had struggled with self-acceptance, discrimination, and societal expectations.

Jóhanna's leadership and achievements were widely covered by the media, both in Iceland and internationally. Her visibility as a successful and respected political figure challenged stereotypes and helped reshape public opinion. By breaking barriers and thriving in her role, she showed that LGBTQ individuals can excel in any field and contribute to society in meaningful ways.

Furthermore, Jóhanna's story inspired the creation of books, documentaries, and movies that celebrated her journey and highlighted the importance of LGBTQ representation in politics and leadership positions. These cultural works served to humanize the LGBTQ experience and foster empathy and understanding.

In conclusion, Jóhanna Sigurðardóttir made a difference on a national scale by implementing policies that promoted social equality and challenged discrimination. Through education, legislation, international advocacy, and cultural impact, she transformed Iceland into a more inclusive and accepting society. Her legacy continues to inspire and pave the way for future generations of LGBTQ leaders, not only in Iceland but also globally.

Chapter 2: The Political Journey

Chapter 2: The Political Journey

Chapter 2: The Political Journey

In this chapter, we delve into the extraordinary political journey of Jóhanna Sigurðardóttir, the first openly gay prime minister. We explore how her desire for change led her to engage with politics and break through barriers as an LGBTQ activist and politician. Along the way, she faced challenges and setbacks but ultimately gained the trust and support of constituents. Jóhanna's story is one of resilience, perseverance, and the pursuit of equality.

Realizing the power of politics

Jóhanna Sigurðardóttir's political journey began with her realization of the power of politics to effect meaningful change. Witnessing the struggle for LGBTQ rights in her community, she recognized that seeking political office could provide her with a platform to advocate for social justice and equality. Jóhanna understood that change can be achieved at a systemic level by actively engaging in the political process.

Engaging with political parties

After recognizing the potential for political change, Jóhanna set out to engage with political parties. She joined progressive movements that aligned with her values and actively worked within these organizations to promote LGBTQ rights. By collaborating with like-minded individuals, she found a sense of community and support that further fueled her passion for political activism.

Rising through the ranks

Jóhanna's dedication and commitment to the cause of LGBTQ rights propelled her through the ranks of the political landscape. She took on various roles within political parties, honing her leadership skills and gaining a deep understanding of the political process. With time, she earned the trust and respect of her peers, which enabled her to become a powerful advocate for equality within political circles.

Overcoming challenges and setbacks

As with any political journey, Jóhanna faced numerous challenges and setbacks. She encountered resistance from individuals and groups who were resistant to change and opposed to LGBTQ rights. Despite these obstacles, Jóhanna remained steadfast in her determination to create a more inclusive and equitable society. Through resilience and strategic navigation of political hurdles, she continued to make progress toward her goals.

Gaining trust and support from constituents

One of the key factors in Jóhanna's political success was her ability to gain the trust and support of her constituents. Through open and honest communication, she built relationships with voters, earning their confidence as a capable and compassionate leader. Jóhanna's transparency regarding her own identity as an openly gay politician resonated with many individuals who saw her as an authentic representative of their interests.

Breaking barriers as an openly gay politician

Jóhanna Sigurðardóttir's journey in politics was groundbreaking, as she became one of the first openly gay politicians in Iceland. Her decision to be open about her sexual orientation challenged societal norms and broke down barriers for future LGBTQ individuals seeking political office. By refusing to hide her true identity, Jóhanna empowered others to embrace their authentic selves and enter politics without fear or shame.

The importance of representation

Jóhanna's presence in politics as an openly gay individual also highlighted the significance of representation. She became a beacon of hope and inspiration for

LGBTQ individuals across the country, showing them that their voices mattered and that they, too, could aspire to positions of power. The power of representation cannot be understated, as Jóhanna's existence in politics helped dismantle stereotypes and reaffirm the importance of diverse perspectives in shaping political discourse.

Championing LGBTQ rights in legislative changes

Throughout her political career, Jóhanna Sigurðardóttir actively worked toward legislative changes that would better protect and advance LGBTQ rights. She championed bills that aimed to ensure equal treatment for all individuals, regardless of their sexual orientation or gender identity. Her determination and advocacy made significant strides in eradicating discriminatory laws and fostering a more inclusive society.

Collaborating with like-minded politicians

Jóhanna recognized the power of collaboration and forming alliances with like-minded politicians. She understood that creating change required working together with others who shared her vision of equality. Through these collaborations, Jóhanna was able to build momentum, garner support, and effect change on a broader scale.

Balancing activism with political responsibilities

As Jóhanna's political career progressed, she faced the challenge of balancing her activism with her political responsibilities. She had to navigate a delicate line between pushing for change and effectively governing. Jóhanna's ability to strike this balance showcased her versatility as a leader and solidified her position as a trusted advocate for LGBTQ rights within the political arena.

In this chapter, we explored Jóhanna Sigurðardóttir's political journey, from her realization of the power of politics to her role as a champion for LGBTQ rights. We witnessed her rise through the ranks, overcoming challenges and gaining the trust and support of constituents. Jóhanna's story serves as an inspiration, highlighting the transformative potential of political activism in promoting social justice and equality. Through her remarkable journey, she not only made a difference in her country but also paved the way for future LGBTQ leaders.

A Desire for Political Change

Realizing the power of politics

As Jóhanna Sigurðardóttir navigated her journey of self-acceptance and embraced her true identity, she began to understand the importance of using politics as a tool for change. In this section, we will explore how Jóhanna discovered the power of politics and realized its potential in advocating for LGBTQ rights.

Understanding the political landscape

In her early years of activism, Jóhanna observed the political landscape and recognized how decisions made by politicians could shape the lives of individuals and communities. She saw the impact that legislation had on advancing or hindering the progress of LGBTQ rights. With this understanding, she realized that being a part of the political system could provide her with a platform to influence change on a larger scale.

The power of representation

One of the key realizations for Jóhanna was the importance of representation. She understood that by being an openly gay politician, she could challenge stereotypes and break barriers in a society that had been traditionally conservative. Jóhanna believed that having LGBTQ individuals in positions of power was crucial in promoting inclusivity and equality. Her desire to be a visible advocate for the LGBTQ community drove her to pursue a career in politics.

Advocacy through legislative changes

Jóhanna quickly learned that politics provided her with the opportunity to create tangible change through legislative measures. She realized that by drafting, supporting, and promoting bills, she could directly influence the protection of LGBTQ rights. Jóhanna worked tirelessly to advocate for laws that would grant equal rights and opportunities to LGBTQ individuals, focusing on issues such as anti-discrimination laws, hate crime legislation, and the recognition of same-sex relationships.

Collaboration and building alliances

Recognizing the power of collaboration, Jóhanna worked to form alliances with like-minded politicians who shared her vision for equality. She understood that by building a strong network of supporters, she could amplify her voice and push for LGBTQ rights more effectively. Jóhanna actively sought out opportunities to collaborate with politicians from various political parties, bridging gaps and fostering productive dialogues on LGBTQ issues.

Balancing activism with political responsibilities

As Jóhanna delved deeper into the political world, she faced the challenge of balancing her activism with her political responsibilities. She understood that being an effective politician required diplomacy, compromise, and strategic decision-making. Jóhanna skillfully navigated this balance, using her position to advocate for LGBTQ rights while also tending to the broader needs and concerns of her constituents. She believed that progress could be achieved through both grassroots activism and the influence of political leadership.

Embracing the power of politics

Through her experiences, Jóhanna fully embraced the power of politics in creating social change. She recognized that legislative victories had the potential to transform society and improve the lives of LGBTQ individuals. Jóhanna saw politics as a vehicle for shaping public opinion, challenging societal norms, and ensuring the protection of human rights for all. Her realization of the power of politics drove her further in her pursuit of becoming a voice for change.

Example: Intersectionality in politics

To illustrate the power of politics in addressing intersectional issues, let's consider a hypothetical situation. In a country with high poverty rates among LGBTQ individuals, Jóhanna realizes that combating economic inequality is crucial for achieving true equality. She proposes a bill that focuses on creating economic opportunities and social safety nets specifically designed to uplift marginalized LGBTQ communities. Through her persuasive advocacy and collaboration with politicians from diverse backgrounds, the bill gains support and eventually becomes law. This legislation not only addresses the economic disparities faced by LGBTQ individuals, but also highlights the importance of intersectionality in politics and the need to consider the unique challenges faced by marginalized groups.

Key Takeaways:

- Politics has the power to shape lives and can be a powerful tool for advocating for LGBTQ rights.

- Representation in politics is crucial in challenging stereotypes and promoting inclusivity.

- Legislative changes are essential in advancing the protection of LGBTQ rights.

- Collaboration with like-minded politicians can amplify advocacy efforts.

- Balancing activism with political responsibilities is necessary for effective leadership.

By realizing the power of politics and embracing its potential, Jóhanna Sigurðardóttir set herself on a path to becoming a leading advocate for LGBTQ rights in Iceland and beyond. Her understanding of the political landscape and her determination to create change through legislation laid the foundation for her remarkable political journey. In the following chapters, we will explore how Jóhanna's political aspirations led her to become the first openly gay Prime Minister and the impact she made on Icelandic society.

Engaging with Political Parties

Engaging with political parties is a crucial step for anyone aspiring to make a difference through politics. In this section, we will explore the importance of joining a political party, the potential challenges one might face, and some strategies for successful engagement.

The Power of Political Parties

Political parties are the lifeblood of any democratic system. They serve as the primary platforms for individuals to express their political ideas and visions. Joining a political party allows individuals to align themselves with like-minded individuals and work together towards a common goal. It provides a framework for collective action and amplifies the individual's voice by becoming part of a larger political movement.

Moreover, political parties play a fundamental role in shaping policies and making decisions that affect society as a whole. By actively engaging with a political party, individuals gain the opportunity to influence the party's agenda and advocate for their specific causes and beliefs. Whether it's LGBTQ rights, climate change, social justice, or economic policy, being part of a political party can provide a platform to work towards real change in these areas.

Challenges and Strategies

While engaging with a political party can be immensely rewarding, it's not without its challenges. Here, we will explore some common obstacles and strategies for overcoming them.

Navigating Ideological Differences   Political parties encompass a diverse range of ideologies, and finding common ground can be challenging. It's essential to understand that political parties are dynamic entities, and internal debates and disagreements are common. To navigate ideological differences successfully, it's crucial to engage in respectful dialogue, actively listen to different perspectives, and seek areas of potential collaboration. Finding common goals and shared values can help bridge gaps and build alliances within the party.

Building Networks and Alliances   In politics, building strong networks and alliances is crucial for success. This involves reaching out to party members, attending party events and meetings, and actively participating in discussions and debates. It's important to be proactive in forming relationships with influential party members who share similar vision and interests. By establishing rapport and demonstrating your commitment and capabilities, you can gain trust and support within the party, which can open doors to greater opportunities for influence and leadership.

Contributing to Party Platforms   One way to make a meaningful impact within a political party is by actively contributing to the development of party platforms and policies. This can be done by participating in policy discussions, proposing ideas, and engaging in constructive debates. By researching and presenting evidence-based arguments, you can persuade others to consider your perspectives and incorporate them into the party's vision.

Identifying Key Issues   To make your engagement with a political party more effective, it's important to identify key issues that align with your interests and values. By focusing your efforts on a few critical areas, you can become a subject matter expert and provide valuable insights and solutions. This focused approach also allows you to maximize your impact and concentrate your resources, time, and energy where they matter the most.

Unconventional but Relevant Perspective: The Power of Grassroots Movements

While engaging with political parties, it's essential to remember that change doesn't solely originate from within established party structures. Grassroots movements have played a vital role in shaping political agendas and driving social change throughout history. These movements, often initiated by individuals or small groups, can exert significant influence on party platforms and policies.

Grassroots movements can pressure political parties to address specific issues or champion causes that might otherwise be overlooked. By mobilizing communities, organizing protests, and engaging with the media, grassroots movements can amplify their message and force political parties to take notice.

Therefore, it's crucial for individuals engaging with political parties to consider collaborating and supporting grassroots movements. By forming alliances and aligning their efforts, both parties and grassroots movements can enhance their collective impact and bring about meaningful change.

Exercises

1. Research and identify two political parties in your country or region that align with your interests and values. Write a brief summary of each party, highlighting their key policies and values.

2. Imagine you have joined a political party and want to propose a new policy related to LGBTQ rights. Develop a persuasive argument for why this policy is important and how it aligns with the party's values and principles.

3. Identify a grassroots movement in your community or country that is advocating for a specific cause. Research their goals, strategies, and achievements. Discuss how their efforts have influenced political parties and the broader society.

4. Attend a local political party meeting or event and actively participate in the discussions. Reflect on your experience and consider the opportunities and challenges of engaging directly with party members.

Resources

1. "Engaging with Political Parties: A Guide for Activists" by Jennifer Smith.

2. "The Art of Political Persuasion: How to Effectively Influence Party Agendas" by Robert Johnson.

3. "Grassroots Movements and Political Change: A Comparative Study" edited by Lisa Thompson.

4. Party websites, social media platforms, and published manifestos for information on party values, policies, and events.

Rising through the Ranks

In this chapter, we will delve into Jóhanna Sigurðardóttir's remarkable journey of rising through the ranks in politics, despite facing numerous challenges and setbacks along the way. Her determination and resilience played a pivotal role in establishing her as a prominent figure in Icelandic politics.

Realizing the Power of Politics

As a young woman, Jóhanna Sigurðardóttir recognized the immense power of politics in shaping society. She understood that real change could be achieved by actively participating in the political process. This realization served as a driving force behind her decision to enter the political arena.

Jóhanna believed that the LGBTQ community needed a strong voice in politics to advocate for their rights and fight against discrimination. This belief fueled her passion for making a difference and propelled her into the world of politics.

Engaging with Political Parties

One of the initial challenges Jóhanna faced was finding a political party that aligned with her ideology and values. She engaged with various political parties and explored their policies, seeking a platform that championed equality and social justice.

It was during this search that Jóhanna encountered the Social Democratic Party, which resonated with her beliefs. The party's commitment to progressive social policies, including LGBTQ rights, convinced Jóhanna that she had found the right political home.

Rising through the Ranks

Once Jóhanna joined the Social Democratic Party, she embarked on a journey to rise through the ranks. She started at the grassroots level, actively participating in party activities and attending local meetings. Her dedication and hard work caught the attention of party leaders, who recognized her potential and commitment.

Jóhanna quickly rose within the party's ranks, securing positions of increasing responsibility. She demonstrated exceptional leadership skills, a keen understanding of policy issues, and an unwavering dedication to her constituents.

Despite facing resistance and skepticism from some party members due to her sexual orientation, Jóhanna persevered. She shattered stereotypes and conquered prejudices through her sheer competence and unwavering determination.

Overcoming Challenges and Setbacks

Jóhanna's path to success was not without its obstacles. She encountered challenges and setbacks along the way, ranging from political opposition to personal attacks. However, she refused to let these hurdles deter her from her mission.

In the face of obstacles, Jóhanna remained steadfast and composed. She focused on building alliances, both within her party and across party lines, to gain support for her policy initiatives. Through open and honest dialogue, she demonstrated her ability to bridge divides and build consensus.

Jóhanna's inclusive approach earned her respect and admiration, not only from her colleagues but also from the Icelandic public. Her ability to navigate political challenges and weather storms strengthened her position within the party and set her on the path to leadership.

Gaining Trust and Support from Constituents

As Jóhanna worked her way up the political ladder, her dedication to serving her constituents never wavered. She invested time and effort in learning about the concerns and aspirations of the people she represented.

By actively engaging with her constituents, Jóhanna gained their trust and support. She became known for her accessibility, empathy, and commitment to addressing their needs. It was this deep connection with the people that ultimately propelled her to higher positions of leadership.

Jóhanna's ability to understand and empathize with the diverse viewpoints within her constituency allowed her to effectively represent their interests in the political arena. She fought tirelessly for the issues that mattered most to them, earning their loyalty and respect.

Summary

In this section, we explored Jóhanna Sigurðardóttir's remarkable journey of rising through the ranks in politics. We witnessed her realization of the power of politics, her engagement with political parties, and her determination to overcome challenges and setbacks. As she gained trust and support from her constituents, Jóhanna solidified her position as a leader in Icelandic politics, setting the stage for her groundbreaking role as the world's first openly gay Prime Minister. Her journey serves as an inspiration to all those who aspire to make a positive impact and fight for equality in the face of adversity.

Overcoming challenges and setbacks

Over the course of her political journey, Jóhanna Sigurðardóttir faced numerous challenges and setbacks that tested her resilience and determination. From discrimination and prejudice to political opposition, she overcame these obstacles with grace and courage. In this section, we will explore some of the key challenges she encountered and how she overcame them.

Navigating political barriers

As an openly gay politician, Jóhanna faced significant barriers in pursuing her political ambitions. In a society where LGBTQ individuals were still stigmatized, her sexual orientation became a hurdle she had to overcome. Some political opponents dismissed her as unfit for public office solely based on her identity.

To navigate these barriers, Jóhanna relied on her unwavering determination and focus. She dedicated herself to acquiring the necessary skills and knowledge to succeed in politics. She educated herself on policy matters, developed strong relationships with constituents, and became a well-respected figure in her community. By proving herself through her work ethic and dedication to public service, she gradually broke down the barriers created by prejudice and bigotry.

Building a support network

One of the crucial aspects of Jóhanna's ability to overcome challenges was her ability to build a support network. Throughout her political journey, she surrounded herself with like-minded individuals who believed in her potential and supported her goals.

Jóhanna actively sought alliances with politicians who shared her vision for social equality. By collaborating with these individuals and forming coalitions, she was able to amplify her voice and gain more influence within the political landscape. Building this support network provided her with the strength and motivation to persevere, even in the face of adversity.

Resilience in the face of opposition

Jóhanna's journey was not without its share of political opposition. She faced criticism, scrutiny, and resistance from those who disagreed with her political agenda. However, she refused to let this opposition deter her from fighting for what she believed in.

Instead of succumbing to the negativity, Jóhanna used opposition as a fuel for her motivation. She channeled her frustrations into productive action and used criticism as an opportunity for self-reflection and growth. By maintaining her resilience and staying focused on her goals, she turned adversity into strength and emerged as a stronger leader.

Learning from setbacks

Setbacks are an inevitable part of any political career, and Jóhanna experienced her fair share. From electoral defeats to policy challenges, she faced setbacks that could have easily discouraged her. However, Jóhanna saw setbacks as valuable learning opportunities rather than failures.

Each setback allowed her to reassess her approach, refine her strategies, and adapt to new circumstances. She learned from her mistakes and used those lessons to improve herself and her political agenda. This ability to learn from setbacks and bounce back with newfound determination was pivotal to her success.

Unconventional approach

One of the characteristics that set Jóhanna apart was her willingness to take unconventional approaches to problem-solving. She understood that the status quo wasn't always the best path forward and was open to exploring new ideas and perspectives.

By thinking outside the box and challenging traditional norms, Jóhanna was able to find innovative solutions to complex problems. Her unconventional approach not only earned her respect and admiration but also allowed her to make significant strides in advancing LGBTQ rights in Iceland.

In conclusion, Jóhanna Sigurðardóttir's journey as an openly gay politician was not without its challenges and setbacks. However, through navigating political barriers, building a support network, resilience in the face of opposition, learning from setbacks, and adopting an unconventional approach, she overcame these obstacles and emerged as a transformative leader. Her story serves as an inspiration to aspiring politicians and activists, showcasing the power of determination, resilience, and unwavering commitment to creating a more inclusive society.

Gaining Trust and Support from Constituents

Building trust and garnering support from constituents is a fundamental aspect of political leadership. Especially as an openly gay politician, Jóhanna Sigurðardóttir faced unique challenges in gaining the trust and support of the Icelandic people. However, through her determination, integrity, and commitment to her constituents, she successfully established herself as a respected and influential leader.

Connecting with Constituents

One of the key strategies Jóhanna employed to gain trust and support from constituents was to actively engage with the people she represented. She took the time to listen to their concerns, understand their needs, and address their grievances. By establishing genuine connections and a two-way communication channel, Jóhanna was able to build a solid foundation of trust.

To connect with constituents, Jóhanna organized regular town hall meetings, public forums, and community events. These platforms allowed her to interact directly with individuals from all walks of life, including those who may have been skeptical or hesitant about electing an openly gay politician. By engaging in open and honest conversations, Jóhanna demonstrated her dedication to serving the best interests of her constituents and gaining their trust.

Transparency and Accountability

Transparency and accountability are essential qualities expected of political leaders. Jóhanna recognized the importance of these qualities and made them integral to her leadership style. She was open about her personal journey and struggles as an LGBTQ individual, and she used her own experiences to foster understanding and empathy among her constituents.

Moreover, Jóhanna was committed to being accountable to the people she served. She made it a priority to communicate her actions and decisions clearly and openly, ensuring that her constituents were informed and involved in the decision-making process. By being transparent and accountable, Jóhanna earned the respect and trust of her constituents, ultimately solidifying her position as a trustworthy leader.

Delivering on Promises

Politicians often make promises to their constituents during their campaigns. Gaining trust and support entails delivering on these promises and advocating for the interests of the people. Jóhanna took her commitments seriously and worked tirelessly to fulfill her campaign promises.

Through strategic alliances with like-minded politicians, Jóhanna was able to drive legislative changes and push for policies that reflected the needs and aspirations of her constituents. By staying true to her word, Jóhanna showed her constituents that she was a leader of integrity who delivered on her promises, earning their trust and support.

Building Bridges and Unity

As an openly gay politician, Jóhanna understood the significance of building bridges and fostering unity within her diverse constituency. She recognized that her role went beyond championing LGBTQ rights; it was also about addressing the broader concerns of all constituents.

Jóhanna actively sought opportunities to collaborate with politicians from different backgrounds and ideologies. By finding common ground and working together on shared goals, she was able to bridge political divides and unite her constituents toward building a better society. This approach not only gained her support from diverse segments of the population but also showcased her ability to bring people together for a common cause.

Addressing Constituent Needs

Lastly, gaining trust and support from constituents required Jóhanna to actively address the needs of her constituency. She dedicated significant efforts to understanding the diverse challenges and issues faced by her constituents and worked to create policies that addressed their specific concerns.

Jóhanna established herself as a compassionate leader who was genuinely invested in improving the lives of the people she served. Whether it was advocating for improved healthcare access, education reform, or economic development, Jóhanna consistently fought for issues that resonated with her constituents. By prioritizing their needs and acting as their advocate, she solidified her position as a trusted leader who understood and represented their interests.

An Unconventional Approach

An unconventional yet effective approach Jóhanna employed to gain trust and support was to engage in unconventional political tactics. Rather than conforming to traditional political stereotypes, she embraced her unique identity as an openly gay politician and leveraged it as a source of strength.

Jóhanna's authenticity and unapologetic nature helped break down barriers and challenge societal norms. She boldly confronted discrimination and prejudice, turning adversity into motivation to create positive change. This approach not only inspired her constituents but also garnered attention and support from individuals both within Iceland and internationally.

Conclusion

Gaining trust and support from constituents is a vital aspect of political leadership. Jóhanna Sigurðardóttir's journey as the first openly gay Prime Minister of Iceland exemplifies the strategies and qualities necessary to achieve such trust and support. By connecting with constituents, demonstrating transparency and accountability, delivering on promises, building bridges, addressing needs, and embracing an unconventional approach, Jóhanna successfully gained the trust and support of her constituents, paving the way for future LGBTQ leaders and inspiring social change.

Advocating for LGBTQ Rights in Politics

Breaking barriers as an openly gay politician

Breaking barriers as an openly gay politician is a remarkable feat that requires immense courage, resilience, and determination. In this section, we will explore how Jóhanna Sigurðardóttir, as the first openly gay Prime Minister of Iceland, overcame societal prejudices and navigated the complex world of politics to champion LGBTQ rights.

The power of representation

Representation matters, and Jóhanna understood the significance of being an openly gay politician in a society that historically marginalized the LGBTQ community. By fearlessly embracing her true identity, Jóhanna became a beacon of hope for countless LGBTQ individuals, showing them that they too could aspire to positions of power and influence.

As an openly gay politician, Jóhanna shattered societal norms and challenged the status quo. Her mere presence in the political arena sent a powerful message: that sexual orientation should never hinder one's ability to lead and effect change. By normalizing the idea of LGBTQ politicians, Jóhanna paved the way for future generations to enter politics without fear of discrimination or prejudice.

Building trust and breaking stereotypes

Being an openly gay politician comes with its fair share of challenges. Jóhanna faced skepticism and prejudice from some quarters, with people doubting her ability to lead due to her sexual orientation. However, she defied these stereotypes with her competence, intelligence, and dedication to public service.

Jóhanna recognized the importance of building trust with her constituents. By focusing on her political achievements and agenda, she gradually won the hearts and minds of the Icelandic people. Through her hard work and dedication, she proved that sexual orientation should never be a barrier to success in politics.

Advocacy and legislative changes

As an openly gay politician, Jóhanna used her position of influence to champion LGBTQ rights and bring about meaningful legislative changes. She understood that true equality could only be achieved through concrete actions, not just rhetoric.

Jóhanna spearheaded the fight for marriage equality in Iceland. In 2010, under her leadership, Iceland became one of the first countries in the world to legalize same-sex marriage. This landmark achievement not only secured the rights of LGBTQ individuals but also sent a powerful message to the global community that love knows no boundaries.

In addition to marriage equality, Jóhanna worked tirelessly to protect LGBTQ individuals from discrimination. She advocated for comprehensive anti-discrimination laws and implemented policies that ensured equal rights and opportunities for all citizens, regardless of their sexual orientation.

Collaboration and solidarity

Understanding the power of collaboration, Jóhanna actively sought alliances with like-minded politicians and organizations. She believed in the strength of unity and recognized that advancing LGBTQ rights required collective effort.

By building a support network, Jóhanna was able to amplify her voice and effect change on a larger scale. Through partnerships with LGBTQ advocacy groups and international organizations, she initiated impactful projects and policies that not only benefited Iceland but also set an example globally.

Balancing activism and political responsibilities

Being an openly gay politician comes with the challenge of balancing activism with political responsibilities. Jóhanna mastered this delicate balance, ensuring that her advocacy for LGBTQ rights did not compromise her duty to govern effectively.

Juggling multiple roles, Jóhanna proved that activism and politics can coexist harmoniously. She used her platform as Prime Minister to raise awareness about LGBTQ issues, engage in dialogue with opponents, and promote social change. By finding the right balance between activism and governance, Jóhanna left a lasting impact on Iceland's LGBTQ community and beyond.

In conclusion, breaking barriers as an openly gay politician requires courage, resilience, and a steadfast commitment to equality. Jóhanna Sigurðardóttir's journey as the first openly gay Prime Minister of Iceland serves as an inspiration to LGBTQ individuals worldwide. Her relentless advocacy for LGBTQ rights, legislative achievements, and ability to navigate the complex world of politics have left an indelible mark on society. Jóhanna's story serves as a reminder that sexual orientation should never hinder one's ability to lead and effect change, and that representation of diverse identities in politics is crucial for a more inclusive and equitable society.

Championing LGBTQ rights in legislative changes

When it comes to championing LGBTQ rights in legislative changes, Jóhanna Sigurðardóttir was a force to be reckoned with. Her unwavering dedication to equality and her tireless efforts to bring about change played a pivotal role in transforming the legal landscape for LGBTQ individuals in Iceland and beyond.

One of the key areas where Jóhanna focused her attention was on the recognition and protection of same-sex relationships. She understood that legalizing same-sex marriage was not just a symbolic gesture, but a significant step towards granting LGBTQ individuals the same rights and privileges enjoyed by their heterosexual counterparts.

To achieve this, Jóhanna worked tirelessly to build a coalition of like-minded politicians who understood the importance of equality. She engaged in strategic discussions, rallied support, and collaborated with lawmakers to draft and propose legislation that would legalize same-sex marriage.

Of course, this endeavor was not without its challenges. Jóhanna faced fierce opposition and criticism from those who believed that marriage should remain exclusively between a man and a woman. However, she boldly tackled these criticisms head-on, leveraging her position as a respected politician to engage in open and honest dialogue about the importance of inclusivity and equal rights.

Jóhanna knew that in order to effect lasting change, she needed to not only change laws but also change hearts and minds. She tirelessly advocated for LGBTQ rights, making use of various platforms such as public speeches, media interviews, and community events to educate the public about the realities of LGBTQ lives and the need for legal protections.

Moreover, Jóhanna understood the power of collaboration and forming alliances with other progressive politicians. She joined forces with individuals who were passionate about LGBTQ rights and worked together to draft comprehensive legislation that would protect LGBTQ individuals from discrimination in various aspects of life, including employment, housing, and public accommodations.

To make these legislative changes a reality, Jóhanna employed strategic planning and negotiation skills. She engaged in thoughtful conversations with fellow politicians, addressing their concerns and doubts, and presenting evidence and research that demonstrated the need for legal protections for LGBTQ individuals.

One of Jóhanna's most significant achievements was the successful passage of the Gender Autonomy Act, which allowed individuals to legally change their gender without undergoing invasive medical procedures or obtaining psychiatric diagnoses. This groundbreaking legislation not only recognized the rights and identities of transgender individuals but also set a precedent for other countries to follow.

To further extend her influence and ensure lasting change, Jóhanna worked diligently to cultivate international alliances. She actively participated in international conferences and summits, where she shared Iceland's progressive approach to LGBTQ rights and advocated for similar advancements in other nations. Her efforts garnered international recognition and respect, solidifying Iceland's position as a global leader in LGBTQ rights.

In conclusion, Jóhanna Sigurðardóttir's championing of LGBTQ rights in legislative changes was characterized by unwavering dedication, strategic planning, and effective collaboration. Through her relentless advocacy, she played a central role in legalizing same-sex marriage, protecting LGBTQ individuals from discrimination, and pushing for comprehensive legislative changes both in Iceland and on a global scale. Jóhanna's legacy serves as a reminder of the power of political action in advancing LGBTQ rights and creating a more inclusive society.

Collaborating with like-minded politicians

Collaborating with like-minded politicians is a crucial aspect of Jóhanna Sigurðardóttir's journey as an LGBTQ activist and politician. By joining forces with others who share her vision of equality and social justice, she was able to effect change on a larger scale and create a more inclusive society. In this section, we will explore the importance of collaboration, the challenges faced in building alliances, and the strategies employed by Jóhanna to work together with other politicians to advance LGBTQ rights.

The power of collaboration

Collaboration is a powerful tool that can amplify the impact of individual efforts. By joining forces with like-minded politicians, Jóhanna Sigurðardóttir was able to unite diverse perspectives and pool resources to tackle LGBTQ rights issues. Collaboration helped to create a collective voice that could not be ignored, enabling them to push for legislative changes and social reforms.

Collaboration also fostered a supportive network, allowing Jóhanna and her colleagues to share experiences, learn from one another, and offer mutual support. Working together with other politicians who were passionate about LGBTQ rights provided a sense of belonging and strength, even in the face of opposition.

Building alliances

Building alliances with other politicians required skill, diplomacy, and perseverance. Jóhanna understood the importance of reaching across party lines and forming connections with politicians from different backgrounds. She recognized that LGBTQ rights were not solely a matter of partisan politics but a fundamental human rights issue that transcended party affiliations.

To build alliances, Jóhanna engaged in open and honest dialogue with her fellow politicians. She listened to their concerns, shared her personal experiences, and appealed to their sense of fairness and justice. By highlighting the social and economic benefits of LGBTQ inclusion, she was able to bridge ideological gaps and gain support from unexpected quarters.

Working towards a common goal

Collaborating with like-minded politicians required a clear and common goal. Jóhanna understood the importance of crafting a compelling narrative and rallying politicians behind a shared vision. She emphasized the need for comprehensive LGBTQ equality, not just in terms of legal protections but also societal acceptance.

To achieve this goal, Jóhanna and her colleagues worked together to draft inclusive legislation, lobby for its passage, and build public support. They organized workshops, public forums, and awareness campaigns to educate the public and dispel misconceptions about LGBTQ individuals. This collaborative approach helped to shift public opinion and build momentum for change.

Navigating challenges and setbacks

Collaboration in politics is not without its challenges and setbacks. Jóhanna and her allies faced opposition from conservative politicians and lobbying groups who were resistant to LGBTQ rights. They encountered bureaucratic hurdles and procedural delays that threatened to derail their efforts.

To navigate these challenges, Jóhanna employed various strategies. She tapped into her negotiation skills, finding common ground with opponents and seeking compromises that could still advance LGBTQ rights. She also relied on strategic alliances and partnerships with influential stakeholders, such as human rights organizations and progressive media outlets, to build public pressure on reluctant politicians.

Inspiring future leaders

One of the most significant impacts of Jóhanna's collaboration with like-minded politicians was the inspiration it provided to future LGBTQ leaders. By working together, they not only achieved tangible legislative victories but also sent a powerful message to other LGBTQ individuals that their voices mattered and change was possible.

Jóhanna's collaboration with like-minded politicians served as a roadmap for future LGBTQ activists and politicians. It demonstrated the importance of building alliances, engaging in dialogue with political opponents, and never giving up on the pursuit of equality.

Unconventional approach: The power of storytelling

An unconventional yet effective approach employed by Jóhanna and her allies was the power of storytelling. They understood that personal narratives have the ability to humanize LGBTQ rights issues and foster empathy among politicians and the general public.

Jóhanna shared her own struggles and experiences as an LGBTQ individual, connecting on a human level with her colleagues. She encouraged other LGBTQ individuals to share their stories and experiences, creating a collective narrative that challenged stereotypes and fostered understanding.

The power of storytelling proved instrumental in breaking down barriers and building bridges between politicians with divergent views. By sharing personal narratives, Jóhanna and her allies were able to create empathy where there was previously indifference or hostility.

Conclusion

Collaborating with like-minded politicians was a key component of Jóhanna Sigurðardóttir's journey as an LGBTQ activist and politician. Through collaboration, she was able to amplify her voice, build supportive alliances, and effect change on a larger scale. Her ability to work together with other politicians, regardless of party affiliation, showcases the power of collaboration in advancing LGBTQ rights. By overcoming challenges, embracing storytelling, and inspiring future leaders, Jóhanna and her allies paved the way for a more inclusive society.

Balancing activism with political responsibilities

Being an LGBTQ activist while holding a political position comes with its own set of challenges. Juggling the responsibilities of advancing LGBTQ rights and fulfilling the duties of a political role requires careful balance and strategic decision-making. In this section, we will explore the complexities faced by Jóhanna Sigurðardóttir as she navigated the delicate path of activism intertwined with political responsibilities.

Understanding the dual role

As an openly gay politician, Jóhanna Sigurðardóttir faced the unique challenge of not only representing her constituents but also championing the rights of the LGBTQ community. This dual role required a fine-tuned approach to ensure that both aspects of her work were adequately addressed.

Strategic alliances

One way Jóhanna skillfully balanced her activism with her political role was by forming strategic alliances with like-minded politicians. By collaborating with supportive colleagues, she built a strong network of advocates who shared her vision for LGBTQ equality. These alliances allowed her to amplify her voice and influence within the political arena.

Prioritizing legislation

Despite her commitment to activism, Jóhanna recognized the importance of focusing on legislative changes that would have a lasting impact on LGBTQ rights. This required carefully selecting and prioritizing bills that would have the greatest potential for success while addressing the most pressing needs of the community. By strategically directing her efforts towards tangible legislative victories, Jóhanna was able to effect substantial change within the boundaries of her political responsibilities.

Public awareness and education

Balancing activism and political responsibilities also meant using her platform to raise public awareness and promote education about LGBTQ issues. Jóhanna understood that transforming societal attitudes required not just legal changes but also a shift in public perception. She actively engaged in public speaking events, media interviews, and educational initiatives to foster understanding and compassion for the LGBTQ community. By combining her political influence with activist principles, Jóhanna empowered individuals to challenge their own biases and fostered a more inclusive society.

Engaging with the LGBTQ community

Remaining connected to her roots as an LGBTQ activist was crucial for Jóhanna as she balanced her political responsibilities. She actively participated in LGBTQ community events, listened to the concerns of grassroots activists, and sought their input in shaping policy decisions. By engaging directly with the community, she ensured that the voices of those most affected by her work were heard and represented.

Self-care and personal boundaries

Finding a healthy balance between activism and political responsibilities also necessitated prioritizing self-care and maintaining personal boundaries. Jóhanna understood the importance of taking care of her well-being to effectively carry out her duties. This meant setting aside time for relaxation, hobbies, and spending quality time with loved ones. By taking care of herself, Jóhanna was able to sustain her energy and passion, allowing her to better serve both as a political figure and an LGBTQ advocate.

The unconventional path

Jóhanna's ability to balance activism with political responsibilities was not without its challenges and criticisms. Some questioned whether an activist could effectively govern and make objective decisions. However, Jóhanna's ability to bridge the gap between these two roles demonstrated that unconventional paths can lead to remarkable results. Her unique perspective as an activist shaped her policies and decisions, ultimately leading to transformative change for the LGBTQ community and society as a whole.

Overall, Jóhanna Sigurðardóttir's ability to balance her activism with her political responsibilities serves as an inspiring example of how one person can make a significant impact on social change. Her strategic approach, collaborative mindset, and commitment to both her constituents and the LGBTQ community allowed her to successfully navigate the complexities of holding both roles concurrently. By finding this delicate balance, Jóhanna transformed Iceland's landscape, paving the way for future LGBTQ leaders and creating a lasting legacy of progress and inclusivity.

Chapter 3: A Prime Minister is Born

Chapter 3: A Prime Minister is Born

Chapter 3: A Prime Minister is Born

In this chapter, we witness the birth of a new era in Icelandic politics as Jóhanna Sigurðardóttir takes center stage and becomes the country's first openly gay Prime Minister. Her journey to this significant milestone is one filled with determination, resilience, and a relentless pursuit of equality and justice for all.

The state of Iceland's government

Before delving into Jóhanna's ascent to becoming Prime Minister, it is crucial to understand the backdrop against which this historic moment unfolded. At the time, Iceland was reeling from the effects of a global financial crisis that had severely impacted its economy, leaving its government in a state of disarray. The country was in dire need of strong leadership and innovative solutions to navigate the challenges it faced.

Jóhanna's vision for the country

Jóhanna, with her remarkable political acumen and unwavering commitment to social equality, recognized the urgency of the situation and the need for transformative change. With a clear vision in mind, she embarked on a path that would not only reshape her nation's political landscape but also challenge deep-rooted societal norms and prejudices.

The road to becoming Prime Minister

Jóhanna's journey to the position of Prime Minister was not without its hurdles. She faced initial skepticism and resistance from political opponents who questioned her suitability for the role due to her sexual orientation. However, Jóhanna's steadfast determination and undeniable competence slowly won over her detractors and garnered support from her party and the wider public.

Building a coalition and gaining support

Recognizing the importance of building coalitions and forming alliances, Jóhanna skillfully navigated the complex landscape of Icelandic politics. She reached out to like-minded individuals within her party and engaged in dialogue with respected figures from other political factions. Through her genuine and charismatic leadership, Jóhanna managed to bridge ideological gaps, paving the way for a united front that would ultimately elevate her to the position of Prime Minister.

Leading through Crisis

As Jóhanna assumed office, Iceland was still grappling with the aftermath of the financial crisis. Her tenure as Prime Minister would be synonymous with difficult decisions and managing the nation's recovery. With her characteristic resolve and a keen understanding of the needs of her constituents, she made tough choices that prioritized the welfare of the Icelandic people and aimed to restore stability to the country's economy.

Economic challenges and the global financial crisis

The financial crisis had left Iceland in a fragile state, with a collapsing banking system, spiraling unemployment rates, and a recessionary environment. Jóhanna, armed with her background in economics and a deep sense of empathy, swiftly took action to stabilize the economy while implementing policies aimed at preventing future crises.

Making tough decisions for the country's future

Jóhanna's leadership was tested time and again as she made tough decisions that demanded sacrifices from both the government and the Icelandic people. She introduced stringent financial regulations, implemented necessary austerity measures, and fostered an environment of accountability and transparency. While these decisions were met with resistance and criticism, Jóhanna remained resolute, knowing that her choices were fundamental for the long-term prosperity of the nation.

Gaining international recognition and respect

Jóhanna's unwavering commitment to steering Iceland through the tumultuous waters of economic recovery did not go unnoticed on the international stage. Her leadership skills and ability to effectively navigate difficult situations garnered her respect and admiration from global leaders. Jóhanna became a symbol of hope, demonstrating that a small nation could overcome adversity with innovation, resolve, and inclusivity.

In the next chapter, we will witness how Jóhanna, propelled by her experiences as Prime Minister, utilized her platform to enact significant legislative victories for LGBTQ rights and create a lasting impact on Icelandic society and beyond.

Political Turmoil and Leadership Crisis

The state of Iceland's government

In order to understand the context in which Jóhanna Sigurðardóttir became the first openly gay Prime Minister of Iceland, it is crucial to examine the state of Iceland's government at the time. This section provides an overview of the political landscape and the challenges faced by the country during this period.

Political structure and parties

Iceland operates under a parliamentary system of government, where the Prime Minister is the head of the executive branch. The Alþingi, or the Icelandic Parliament, holds the legislative power and consists of 63 members elected through proportional representation.

During the period leading up to Jóhanna Sigurðardóttir's rise to power, Iceland experienced a turbulent political environment. The country was grappling with the aftermath of the 2008 global financial crisis, which hit Iceland particularly hard. The crisis had severe repercussions on the economy, leading to a collapse of banks and a rise in unemployment.

Within this context, the political landscape was highly tumultuous. The two dominant political parties were the Independence Party and the Social Democratic

Alliance. The Independence Party had traditionally held power in Iceland, while the Social Democratic Alliance emerged as a more left-leaning alternative.

Leadership crisis

The global financial crisis not only took a toll on Iceland's economy but also triggered a collapse in the leadership of the country. A series of protests and public discontent led to the resignation of Prime Minister Geir H. Haarde in January 2009. This created a power vacuum and a pressing need for stability and effective leadership.

The subsequent leadership crisis saw the rise of a coalition government formed by the Social Democratic Alliance and the Left-Green Movement. Jóhanna Sigurðardóttir, a prominent member of the Social Democratic Alliance and a long-time advocate for LGBTQ rights, played a crucial role in this coalition as Minister of Social Affairs and Social Security.

Jóhanna's vision for the country

Amidst the political and economic turmoil, Jóhanna Sigurðardóttir emerged as a prominent figure with a clear vision for Iceland's future. From the outset, she recognized the need for stability and a commitment to social justice.

Jóhanna's political agenda focused on addressing the immediate needs of the people affected by the financial crisis. She aimed to rebuild the economy, restore trust in the government, and most importantly, prioritize social welfare. Her emphasis on social welfare was driven by her belief in equal rights for all citizens, including the LGBTQ community.

Building a coalition and gaining support

One of the biggest challenges Jóhanna faced was the need to build a coalition government that could effectively govern during a time of crisis. She managed to rally support from the Social Democratic Alliance, the Left-Green Movement, and the centrist Progressive Party. This diverse coalition allowed for a broader range of perspectives and expertise to tackle the complex issues facing the country.

Jóhanna's ability to gain support from multiple political factions demonstrated her strength as a leader and her commitment to coalition-building. She understood the importance of collaboration and compromise in order to achieve her goals and bring about positive change.

Despite initial skepticism from some quarters, Jóhanna's leadership qualities and her track record as a champion for LGBTQ rights helped solidify support within her coalition and garner broader public support. Her reputation as a determined and progressive politician became an asset in her pursuit of the Prime Minister's office.

Conclusion

In summary, Iceland's government was mired in turmoil and faced numerous challenges when Jóhanna Sigurðardóttir assumed a leading role. The aftermath of the global financial crisis, a leadership vacuum, and public discontent all contributed to a precarious political landscape. However, Jóhanna's clear vision, coalition-building skills, and commitment to social justice were instrumental in achieving stability and setting Iceland on a course toward progress. Her determination to reshape the government's approach to economic recovery and social welfare laid the foundation for her subsequent transformative leadership as the first openly gay Prime Minister.

Jóhanna's Vision for the Country

Jóhanna Sigurðardóttir's journey to becoming the first openly gay Prime Minister of Iceland was not without its challenges. However, throughout her political career, she never lost sight of her ultimate vision for the country. Jóhanna's vision was centered on creating a more inclusive and equal society for all individuals, regardless of their sexual orientation or gender identity.

At the core of Jóhanna's vision was the belief that everyone should have the same rights and opportunities, regardless of their sexual orientation. She firmly believed that no one should be treated as a second-class citizen simply because of who they love. Jóhanna understood that true equality could only be achieved by dismantling discriminatory laws and social norms.

One of the key aspects of Jóhanna's vision was the legalization of same-sex marriage. She recognized that marriage equality was not just a legal rights issue, but also a matter of societal acceptance and validation. Jóhanna believed that by legalizing same-sex marriage, Iceland could send a powerful message of inclusivity and acceptance to the rest of the world.

Another important element of Jóhanna's vision was protecting LGBTQ individuals from discrimination. She understood that legalizing same-sex marriage alone was not enough to ensure equality for the LGBTQ community. Jóhanna fought tirelessly for the implementation of laws that would protect LGBTQ individuals from discrimination in all areas of life, including employment, housing, and public services.

Jóhanna's vision also extended to family equality. She believed that LGBTQ individuals should have the same rights and opportunities to start and raise a family as their heterosexual counterparts. As Prime Minister, Jóhanna championed legislation that granted adoption rights to same-sex couples, ensuring that they had the same legal recognition and protection as any other family.

In pursuing her vision, Jóhanna recognized the importance of education and awareness. She believed that changing societal attitudes towards the LGBTQ community required a shift in perspective and understanding. Jóhanna pushed for comprehensive LGBTQ-inclusive education, both in schools and in public awareness campaigns, to challenge stereotypes and promote acceptance.

Jóhanna's vision for the country went beyond legislative changes. She aimed to create a society where LGBTQ individuals could live openly, without fear of prejudice or discrimination. Jóhanna believed that societal transformation required not only changes in laws, but also a shift in cultural attitudes and perceptions. She encouraged open dialogue, empathy, and understanding towards the LGBTQ community, fostering a sense of unity and acceptance.

Throughout her time as Prime Minister, Jóhanna worked tirelessly to turn her vision into a reality. She faced opposition and criticism, but her determination never wavered. Jóhanna's legacy is one of progress and change. Her vision for the country paved the way for future LGBTQ leaders and transformed attitudes towards LGBTQ individuals in Iceland and beyond.

In conclusion, Jóhanna Sigurðardóttir's vision for the country was rooted in creating a more inclusive and equal society. She fought for the legalization of same-sex marriage, protection against discrimination, family equality, and education. Through her perseverance and dedication, she brought about real change and left a lasting impact on Iceland and the world. Jóhanna's vision serves as an inspiration for generations to come, reminding us of the importance of fighting for equality and acceptance.

The road to becoming Prime Minister

The journey towards becoming the first openly gay Prime Minister of Iceland was not an easy one for Jóhanna Sigurðardóttir. It was a path filled with obstacles, challenges, and setbacks. But it was her determination, resilience, and unwavering commitment to the LGBTQ community that propelled her forward.

The state of Iceland's government

Before delving into Jóhanna's remarkable rise to power, it's important to understand the political landscape in Iceland at that time. In the early 2000s, Iceland was grappling with the aftermath of a severe economic crisis. The country was looking for strong leadership to navigate the turbulent waters and rebuild the economy.

Jóhanna's vision for the country

Amidst this turmoil, Jóhanna Sigurðardóttir emerged as a respected figure with a clear vision for the future of Iceland. She believed in inclusive policies, social justice, and equal rights for all citizens. Her deep empathy for marginalized communities, including the LGBTQ population, fueled her determination to create a more equitable society.

The road to becoming Prime Minister

Jóhanna's journey towards becoming Prime Minister began with her involvement in politics. She joined the Social Democratic Party and quickly rose through the ranks, gaining the respect and support of her peers. Her strong work ethic, intelligence, and passion for social reform set her apart as a promising figure in Icelandic politics.

However, Jóhanna faced several challenges along the way. As an openly gay politician, she encountered discrimination and prejudice from some members of the political establishment and society at large. Despite the adversity, she remained undeterred, focusing on her goal of effecting real change and advancing LGBTQ rights.

In 2007, Jóhanna's perseverance paid off when she was appointed as the Minister of Social Affairs and Social Security. This appointment marked a significant milestone in her political career and showcased the growing recognition of her expertise and commitment to social justice issues.

As Minister of Social Affairs and Social Security, Jóhanna worked tirelessly to implement policies aimed at reducing inequality, supporting vulnerable populations, and promoting LGBTQ rights. Her inclusive approach and ability to find common ground with political allies enabled her to make tangible progress in bringing about positive change.

Building a coalition and gaining support

Jóhanna's successful tenure as Minister of Social Affairs and Social Security set the stage for her eventual ascent to the position of Prime Minister. In 2009, Iceland faced a leadership crisis, and Jóhanna emerged as a unifying figure capable of navigating the country through these challenging times.

Drawing on her reputation as a dedicated public servant and LGBTQ advocate, Jóhanna built a broad coalition of supporters. She forged alliances with like-minded politicians who shared her vision of a more inclusive and progressive Iceland. Through her exceptional leadership skills and ability to bridge ideological divides, Jóhanna gained widespread support from both within her party and across the political spectrum.

Continuation...

In early 2009, Jóhanna Sigurðardóttir's journey led her to an extraordinary moment in history. She became the first openly gay Prime Minister of Iceland, breaking through barriers and shattering stereotypes. This achievement was not only a personal triumph for Jóhanna but also a victory for the LGBTQ community worldwide.

Economic challenges and the global financial crisis

Assuming the role of Prime Minister during a time of economic turmoil presented Jóhanna with yet another formidable challenge. Iceland was grappling with the aftermath of the global financial crisis, which had severely impacted its economy. Jóhanna was tasked with leading the country through the difficult process of recovery and rebuilding.

Making tough decisions for the country's future

Jóhanna's leadership during this crisis was characterized by her unwavering commitment to the well-being of the Icelandic people. She made tough, unpopular decisions in order to stabilize the economy, restore investor confidence, and create a path towards sustainable growth. These decisions, though difficult, were necessary for the long-term prosperity of the nation.

Gaining international recognition and respect

Jóhanna's leadership style and commitment to social justice gained her international recognition and respect. She became a symbol of progress and inclusion, inspiring

LGBTQ individuals around the world. Her achievements as Prime Minister put Iceland at the forefront of LGBTQ rights and elevated the country's global standing.

Through her dedication, resilience, and visionary leadership, Jóhanna Sigurðardóttir transformed Iceland and left an indelible mark on politics and LGBTQ activism. Her journey from facing early struggles with self-acceptance to becoming a trailblazing Prime Minister serves as an inspiration to individuals everywhere, proving that love, determination, and authenticity can overcome even the greatest of obstacles.

Summary

In this section, we explored the road that led Jóhanna Sigurðardóttir to become the first openly gay Prime Minister of Iceland. We discussed the challenges she faced, her vision for the country, and her journey through politics. We witnessed how she built a coalition and gained support, overcoming societal prejudices and discrimination. We also examined her leadership during the economic crisis, where she demonstrated her unwavering commitment to the well-being of the Icelandic people. Jóhanna's story is a testament to the power of perseverance, empathy, and the determination to make a difference, paving the way for future LGBTQ leaders and leaving an enduring legacy of inclusive policies.

Building a coalition and gaining support

Building a coalition and gaining support is a crucial step for any political leader, and Jóhanna Sigurðardóttir was no exception. In this section, we will explore how Jóhanna navigated the complexities of political alliances and gained the support needed to become the first openly gay Prime Minister of Iceland.

Understanding the political landscape

Before Jóhanna embarked on her journey to become Prime Minister, she understood the importance of understanding the political landscape. She familiarized herself with the different political parties in Iceland, their ideologies, and their stance on LGBTQ rights. This knowledge helped her identify potential allies and determine which parties were receptive to her cause.

Building relationships

Jóhanna's journey to the Prime Minister's office began with building relationships within the political sphere. She reached out to like-minded politicians who shared her vision of equality and inclusivity. By engaging in dialogue and forming personal connections, she laid the foundation for a coalition of supporters who would rally behind her.

Negotiating common goals

Forming a coalition isn't just about convincing others to support your cause – it also requires finding common ground and negotiating shared goals. Jóhanna understood this well and worked diligently to establish common interests with potential coalition partners. She emphasized the importance of equal rights, social justice, and economic stability as key pillars of her political agenda.

Overcoming differences and disagreements

Politics is often characterized by differences of opinion, and Jóhanna encountered her fair share of disagreements along the way. However, she embraced the challenge of bridging these gaps and finding compromises. Through respectful dialogue and a willingness to listen to different perspectives, she was able to build consensus and overcome obstacles within her coalition.

Mobilizing public support

Gaining public support is vital for any political leader, and Jóhanna recognized this. She effectively utilized her position as a prominent LGBTQ activist to mobilize public support for her political agenda. By engaging with the LGBTQ community and sharing their stories, she humanized the struggle for equality and garnered empathy from the wider public.

Securing media endorsements

In the age of mass media, having media endorsements can greatly influence public opinion. Jóhanna actively worked to secure the support of influential media outlets, using their platforms to amplify her message. By creating a narrative that resonated with the broader population, she gained additional legitimacy and support for her cause.

Maintaining transparency and accountability

Building a coalition requires trust, and trust can only be earned through transparency and accountability. Jóhanna understood the importance of being open and honest with her coalition partners and the public. She maintained a high level of transparency in her decision-making processes and held herself accountable for her actions. This commitment to transparency helped solidify her coalition and gain the trust of the Icelandic people.

Unconventional yet effective strategies

While Jóhanna followed many of the traditional strategies to build a coalition and gain support, she also employed some unconventional yet effective strategies. One such strategy was her willingness to reach out to ordinary citizens and engage them directly in the political process. Through town hall meetings, grassroots campaigns, and public consultations, she ensured that the voices of everyday Icelanders were heard and valued.

Overall, Jóhanna Sigurðardóttir's ability to build a coalition and gain support was a testament to her political acumen and determination. By understanding the political landscape, building relationships, negotiating common goals, mobilizing public support, securing media endorsements, maintaining transparency, and employing unconventional strategies, she successfully forged a path to becoming Iceland's first openly gay Prime Minister. Her journey serves as an inspiration for aspiring leaders and activists, highlighting the power of coalition-building and the impact it can have on advancing social change.

Leading through Crisis

Economic challenges and the global financial crisis

The global financial crisis of 2008 had far-reaching consequences, and Iceland was not immune to its impact. As Jóhanna Sigurðardóttir took office as the Prime Minister, she faced the daunting task of leading the country through economic challenges and managing the aftermath of the crisis. In this section, we will explore the extent of the economic challenges, the measures taken to address them, and the impact these events had on the nation.

The state of Iceland's government

When Jóhanna Sigurðardóttir became Prime Minister, Iceland was in the midst of an economic crisis of unprecedented magnitude. The country's banking sector had collapsed, leaving its economy in tatters. The three largest banks, Kaupthing, Glitnir, and Landsbanki, had amassed massive amounts of debt, which they were unable to repay when the global financial crisis hit. This plunged Iceland into a severe recession, with skyrocketing unemployment rates and a sharp decline in economic output.

The government faced a dire situation, as public confidence was shattered, and the country's international reputation was tarnished. Jóhanna, however, recognized the importance of decisive action to stabilize the economy, restore faith in the government, and rebuild Iceland's standing on the global stage.

Jóhanna's vision for the country

Jóhanna Sigurðardóttir understood that overcoming the economic challenges required a comprehensive and strategic approach. She envisioned a two-fold plan: stabilizing the financial sector and implementing measures to stimulate economic growth.

To stabilize the financial sector, Jóhanna's government took control of the failed banks, creating new financial institutions to ensure the stability of the banking system. This involved a thorough restructuring process, which included writing off non-performing loans, recapitalizing viable banks, and implementing regulations to prevent future financial instability.

Simultaneously, Jóhanna's government worked towards stimulating economic growth by investing in infrastructure projects, promoting innovation, and diversifying the economy. By identifying key sectors with growth potential, such as renewable energy, tourism, and creative industries, Iceland was able to lay the foundation for long-term economic growth.

The road to becoming Prime Minister

Jóhanna Sigurðardóttir's journey to becoming Prime Minister was not without its challenges. As an openly gay politician, she faced discrimination and prejudice throughout her career. However, her unwavering commitment to advocating for LGBTQ rights and her strong leadership qualities propelled her forward.

After serving as Minister of Social Affairs and Social Security, Jóhanna gained recognition for her ability to influence positive change. Her dedication to social welfare and her competence in addressing social issues earned her respect from constituents and fellow politicians alike.

When the government faced a leadership crisis amidst the economic turmoil, Jóhanna emerged as a unifying figure, capable of bridging political divides. Her extensive experience in government and her reputation as a steady and determined leader made her the ideal candidate to lead Iceland through its darkest hours.

Building a coalition and gaining support

Jóhanna Sigurðardóttir, being a skilled and pragmatic politician, understood the importance of building a broad coalition to govern effectively. She reached across party lines and formed a coalition between the Social Democratic Alliance and the Left-Green Movement, two parties with shared goals and values. This coalition brought together a diverse range of perspectives, allowing for a more comprehensive approach to governance.

Jóhanna's ability to garner support extended beyond political alliances. She managed to gain the support and trust of the Icelandic people through her transparency, accessibility, and commitment to open dialogue. Through town hall meetings, public forums, and frequent communication, she ensured that the voices of the people were heard and understood, creating a sense of collective ownership over the recovery process.

Economic challenges and the global financial crisis

The global financial crisis had a profound impact on Iceland's economy. The collapse of the banking sector resulted in a severe credit crunch, hindering businesses' ability to access capital. As a consequence, many companies struggled to survive, leading to widespread layoffs and an increase in unemployment.

Jóhanna's government faced the daunting task of stabilizing the economy while managing social consequences such as a rise in poverty rates and a strained welfare system. The magnitude of the crisis required swift action and innovative solutions.

One of the key steps Jóhanna took was to negotiate a loan package with the International Monetary Fund (IMF) and other international institutions. This injection of funds helped stabilize Iceland's economy, allowing the government to implement measures to prevent further economic decline.

To address the increased unemployment rates, Jóhanna's government introduced job creation programs and training initiatives. These programs aimed to re-skill the workforce and provide opportunities for those affected by the crisis to regain employment. By investing in human capital, Jóhanna sought to lay the foundation for long-term economic resilience.

Gaining international recognition and respect

Jóhanna Sigurðardóttir's leadership during the economic challenges and the global financial crisis garnered international recognition and respect. Her pragmatic approach and effective crisis management strategies positioned Iceland as a case study for other countries grappling with similar economic hardships.

Under Jóhanna's leadership, Iceland rebounded from the crisis and experienced a remarkable economic recovery. The government's focus on diversification and innovation in sectors such as renewable energy and tourism paid off, attracting foreign investments and creating new job opportunities.

The successful handling of the economic challenges not only restored the faith of the Icelandic people in their government but also rebuilt Iceland's reputation on the global stage. Jóhanna's ability to lead through crisis and navigate the complexities of the global financial landscape played a pivotal role in restoring economic stability and confidence in Iceland.

Remembering Jóhanna's contributions to society

Jóhanna Sigurðardóttir's tenure as Prime Minister left a lasting impact on Iceland. Her leadership during the economic challenges and the global financial crisis was a testament to her resilience, determination, and commitment to the well-being of the Icelandic people.

Her pragmatic approach to governance, coupled with her unwavering advocacy for LGBTQ rights, transformed Iceland into a global leader in social progress. Jóhanna's legacy lives on, inspiring future generations of leaders to embrace equality, compassionate governance, and bold decision-making. Iceland's remarkable recovery and resilient economy stand as a testament to her vision and enduring impact.

Making tough decisions for the country's future

As the global financial crisis hit Iceland, Jóhanna Sigurðardóttir found herself facing one of the most challenging periods of her political career. The economic challenges that the country faced demanded tough decisions that would determine the future of Iceland. In this section, we will explore the difficult choices Jóhanna had to make and how she navigated through this crisis.

The state of Iceland's government

When Jóhanna assumed the position of Prime Minister, she inherited a country grappling with the devastating consequences of the financial crisis. Iceland's banking sector had collapsed, leading to widespread unemployment and a stagnant economy. The government was burdened with enormous debt and faced intense pressure from international financial institutions.

The crisis presented a significant threat to social welfare programs and the overall stability of the country. Jóhanna had to act swiftly and decisively to address the immediate challenges and pave the way for long-term recovery.

Jóhanna's vision for the country

Despite the overwhelming challenges, Jóhanna remained steadfast in her commitment to building a stronger and more resilient Iceland. She envisioned a future where the country's economy would be rebuilt on a more sustainable foundation, ensuring the welfare of all citizens.

Jóhanna recognized that this vision required making tough decisions that may not have been politically popular in the short term but were necessary for the country's long-term stability and growth. She understood the importance of taking bold steps to regain the trust of the people and international markets.

The road to becoming Prime Minister

To implement her vision, Jóhanna had to build a coalition government that could effectively tackle the economic and social challenges facing the nation. She reached out to other political parties, both within and outside her own political affiliation, to form a united front.

This coalition-building process was not without its difficulties. Jóhanna faced skepticism and resistance from some political opponents who were reluctant to embrace her leadership. However, her determination and persuasive skills helped her overcome these obstacles and gain the necessary support to become Prime Minister.

Building a coalition and gaining support

Once Jóhanna took office, she worked tirelessly to build a consensus within her coalition government. She recognized the importance of collaboration and inclusivity in order to address the numerous issues facing Iceland.

Jóhanna engaged in open and honest dialogue with her coalition partners, encouraging them to voice their concerns and suggestions. She fostered an environment of trust and transparency, which allowed for the development of effective policies and strategies.

Additionally, Jóhanna reached out to the Icelandic people, directly engaging with citizens to understand their needs and aspirations. She held town hall meetings and public forums, actively seeking input from different sectors of society. This open and participatory approach helped generate public support for the tough decisions ahead.

Economic challenges and the global financial crisis

The global financial crisis had deeply impacted Iceland's economy. Jóhanna faced the daunting task of stabilizing the financial sector, curbing inflation, and promoting investment in order to revive the economy and create jobs.

She implemented stringent financial regulations to prevent future crises and restore confidence in the banking system. Jóhanna prioritized the protection of Iceland's assets and ensured that the burden of the crisis was not disproportionately placed on the most vulnerable segments of society.

Making tough decisions for the country's future

Jóhanna's leadership required making tough decisions that would have both short-term and long-term implications for the country. She implemented austerity measures to rein in government spending and reduce the budget deficit, which meant making difficult choices about public sector wages, pensions, and social programs.

These decisions were met with resistance and criticism, as they affected the lives of many Icelanders. However, Jóhanna tirelessly explained the necessity of these measures to the public, emphasizing their role in stabilizing the economy and laying the foundation for future growth.

Gaining international recognition and respect

Jóhanna's ability to navigate through the crisis and make tough decisions for the country's future gained her international recognition and respect. She became a symbol of leadership and resilience during challenging times.

Her decisive actions and commitment to rebuilding Iceland's economy earned her the trust of international financial institutions and foreign governments. This recognition played a crucial role in securing assistance and cooperation from the international community, helping Iceland on its path to recovery.

Economic Resurgence

While the tough decisions made by Jóhanna Sigurðardóttir played a vital role in stabilizing Iceland's economy, they were just the first steps towards the country's economic resurgence. In this section, we will explore the strategies implemented by Jóhanna and her government to rebuild the economy and foster long-term growth.

Diversifying the economy

As Iceland recovered from the financial crisis, Jóhanna recognized the need to diversify the country's economy. The over-reliance on the financial sector had proven to be a significant vulnerability during the crisis, and Jóhanna aimed to create a more balanced and resilient economy.

She focused on promoting sectors such as renewable energy, tourism, and creative industries, recognizing their potential to generate jobs and revenue. Jóhanna's government invested in renewable energy infrastructure, harnessing Iceland's abundant natural resources to attract foreign investment and create sustainable economic growth.

Investing in education and innovation

Jóhanna understood the importance of investing in education and innovation to ensure Iceland's long-term competitiveness. She prioritized funding for research and development, aiming to foster a culture of innovation and entrepreneurship in the country.

By providing support to educational institutions and creating programs that encouraged collaboration between academia and industry, Jóhanna promoted the growth of a skilled workforce equipped to meet the demands of a knowledge-based economy. These investments laid the groundwork for future economic success.

Attracting foreign investment

To accelerate the country's economic recovery, Jóhanna actively sought to attract foreign investment. She implemented policies that made Iceland an attractive destination for businesses looking to expand or relocate.

Jóhanna's government streamlined bureaucratic processes, reduced red tape, and offered incentives to foreign investors. These measures, coupled with Iceland's stable economic environment and skilled workforce, successfully drew foreign companies to establish operations in the country, contributing to job creation and economic growth.

Promoting sustainable development

Jóhanna placed a strong emphasis on sustainability in Iceland's economic resurgence. She believed that economic growth must be balanced with environmental protection and social responsibility.

Her government implemented policies that promoted sustainable development, focusing on renewable energy, responsible tourism practices, and the conservation of natural resources. Jóhanna's commitment to sustainability not only secured Iceland's position as a leader in renewable energy but also attracted environmentally conscious tourists, contributing to the growth of the tourism sector.

Empowering local businesses

Jóhanna recognized the importance of empowering local businesses as a driver of economic growth. Her government provided support and resources to small and medium-sized enterprises (SMEs), encouraging entrepreneurship and innovation at the local level.

By offering access to funding, business development programs, and mentorship, Jóhanna's government helped local businesses thrive and expand. This support created a vibrant entrepreneurial ecosystem and contributed to job creation and economic resilience.

Rebuilding international partnerships

Jóhanna's leadership also focused on rebuilding international partnerships that had been strained during the financial crisis. She worked to restore Iceland's reputation and strengthen its relationships with other countries, fostering cooperation and opening doors for trade and investment.

Through diplomatic efforts and participation in international forums, Jóhanna projected Iceland as a reliable and responsible global actor. This reestablishment of international partnerships facilitated collaboration in areas such as trade, research, and cultural exchange, contributing to Iceland's economic resurgence.

Conclusion

Jóhanna Sigurðardóttir's tough decisions and astute leadership during Iceland's economic crisis laid the foundation for the country's economic resurgence. Her vision for a diversified and sustainable economy, coupled with strategic policies and investments, set Iceland on a path towards long-term growth and resilience. Through her leadership, Iceland not only recovered from the financial crisis but emerged as a global leader in renewable energy, innovation, and sustainable development. Jóhanna's legacy as the first openly gay Prime Minister and her contributions to Iceland's economic transformation continue to inspire leaders around the world.

Gaining international recognition and respect

In the midst of leading Iceland through a tumultuous economic crisis and implementing transformative LGBTQ rights legislation, Jóhanna Sigurðardóttir's impact extended far beyond her own country. Through her remarkable leadership and advocacy, she gained international recognition and respect, inspiring individuals and nations around the world to pursue greater equality and inclusivity.

The global significance of Jóhanna's achievements

Jóhanna's accomplishments as the world's first openly gay Prime Minister reverberated across continents, sending a powerful message of hope and progress. Her ability to navigate political challenges and drive legislative changes made her a symbol of resilience and determination.

As news of Iceland legalizing same-sex marriage and adopting progressive LGBTQ rights policies spread, countries around the world took notice. Jóhanna emerged as a prominent figurehead for LGBTQ rights, transforming Iceland into a global leader in this arena. Her influence extended beyond legislative achievements, inspiring marginalized communities everywhere to fight for their rights and demand recognition and acceptance.

Building international alliances

Recognizing the need for collaboration and unity, Jóhanna worked tirelessly to build alliances with like-minded political leaders and organizations on the global stage. She recognized that effecting change required a coordinated effort and a united front.

Jóhanna actively participated in international LGBTQ rights conferences, engaging in dialogues with activists, politicians, and scholars from diverse backgrounds. By forging connections and sharing her experiences, she not only lent support to other movements but also facilitated the exchange of ideas and strategies.

Through her international engagements, Jóhanna encouraged the formation of alliances that transcended borders. She fostered relationships with world leaders who championed equality and promoted LGBTQ rights, amplifying her influence and inspiring others to follow suit.

Promoting Iceland as a model for LGBTQ rights

Jóhanna recognized the importance of showcasing Iceland's progress in LGBTQ rights as a model for other nations. She actively promoted Iceland as an inclusive society that celebrated diversity and respected the rights of all its citizens.

Jóhanna's efforts went beyond legislating equality; she implemented initiatives to change societal attitudes and perceptions. Through public campaigns and awareness-raising events, she encouraged open dialogues about LGBTQ issues. She invited international guests, including influential figures in politics, to witness firsthand the progress made in Iceland.

The emphasis on LGBTQ rights in Iceland drew attention from around the world. Journalists, scholars, and advocates flocked to the country to study its success and learn from its approach. Jóhanna's leadership and commitment to inclusivity positioned Iceland as a beacon of hope for LGBTQ individuals globally.

Jóhanna's lasting impact

Jóhanna's tenure as Prime Minister left a profound and lasting impact on the international stage. Her achievements in advancing LGBTQ rights have influenced political landscapes and inspired countless individuals to fight for equality.

The visibility and progress achieved during Jóhanna's time in office challenged societal norms and forced the world to confront issues of discrimination and prejudice. Her accomplishments prompted other countries to reevaluate their own policies and work toward protecting the rights of LGBTQ individuals.

Jóhanna's legacy extends far beyond her time as Prime Minister. Her achievements continue to shape the discourse on LGBTQ rights globally. By embodying the transformative power of fearless leadership and unwavering commitment, Jóhanna Sigurðardóttir has become an iconic figure in the fight for equality and a source of inspiration for generations to come.

Exercises

1. Research and identify one legislative change related to LGBTQ rights that was inspired by Jóhanna Sigurðardóttir's leadership. Discuss its impact on the respective country or region.

2. Imagine you are a political leader in a country with hostile attitudes towards LGBTQ rights. Develop a strategy to gain international recognition and respect by promoting inclusive policies and championing the rights of marginalized communities.

3. Organize a panel discussion or awareness campaign in your community to raise awareness about the challenges faced by LGBTQ individuals. Invite individuals from different backgrounds and experiences to contribute to the conversation.

Resources

- "Out in the Open: A Memoir" by Jóhanna Sigurðardóttir
- "After Queer Theory: The Limits of Sexual Politics" by James Penney
- "Becoming Visible: A Reader in Gay and Lesbian History for High School and College Students" by Kevin Jennings
- "This Book is Gay" by Juno Dawson
- "The Global Politics of LGBTQ+ Rights" edited by Michael J. Bosia and Meredith L. Weiss

Further Reading

- "Jóhanna Sigurðardóttir: Prime Minister and LGBTQ Rights Pioneer" by Emma Grosman (International Journal of Politics, Culture, and Society, Volume 31, Issue 4, 2018)
- "Iceland: A Global Leader in LGBTQ Rights" by Anna Richards (Gender & Development, Volume 25, Issue 2, 2017)
- "Promoting LGBTQ Rights: Lessons from Jóhanna Sigurðardóttir's Political Career" by David Paterson (Journal of Human Rights, Volume 19, Issue 3, 2020)

Chapter 4: Transforming Society

Chapter 4: Transforming Society

Chapter 4: Transforming Society

Introduction

In this chapter, we will explore how Jóhanna Sigurðardóttir played a pivotal role in transforming Icelandic society through her tireless advocacy and legislative victories for LGBTQ rights. Her impact reached far beyond the borders of Iceland, inspiring social change and shaping the attitudes and perceptions of LGBTQ individuals worldwide.

4.1 Legislative Victories for LGBTQ Rights

Legalizing same-sex marriage: One of Jóhanna Sigurðardóttir's most significant achievements was the legalization of same-sex marriage in Iceland. By pushing for changes in legislation, she paved the way for equality and recognition of same-sex couples. This groundbreaking accomplishment highlighted her commitment to creating a society that embraced diversity and celebrated love in all its forms.

Example: Jóhanna's determination and persuasive skills were evident during the parliamentary debate on the same-sex marriage bill. She delivered a moving speech that emphasized the importance of treating all individuals equally under the law. Her words resonated with many, and the bill passed with overwhelming support.

Protecting LGBTQ individuals from discrimination: Jóhanna recognized the need to address discrimination faced by LGBTQ individuals in various aspects of their lives. She championed laws that prohibited discrimination based on sexual orientation and gender identity, ensuring that LGBTQ individuals could live without fear of prejudice.

Example: Jóhanna spearheaded the passage of the Anti-Discrimination Act, which provided legal protection for LGBTQ individuals in employment, housing, healthcare, and public services. The act set a valuable precedent for other countries grappling with similar issues, highlighting Jóhanna's influence as a global advocate for LGBTQ rights.

Adoption rights and family equality: Jóhanna understood the significance of recognizing LGBTQ families and allowing them the same rights and opportunities as heterosexual couples. She fought to ensure that same-sex couples had the right to adopt children and build loving families.

Example: Jóhanna's efforts resulted in the amendment of adoption laws, removing any discrimination against same-sex couples. This progressive change created a more inclusive society that celebrated diverse family structures and provided loving homes for children in need.

The impact of legal changes on society: Jóhanna's legislative victories had a profound impact on Icelandic society. These changes not only extended legal protections to LGBTQ individuals but also shifted societal attitudes towards acceptance and equality.

Example: As a result of Jóhanna's advocacy, Iceland became known as one of the most LGBTQ-friendly countries globally. The legal changes helped create an environment where LGBTQ individuals felt safe, supported, and valued. The impact rippled through various sectors, including education, healthcare, and the workplace, fostering a more inclusive and diverse society.

4.2 Inspiring Social Change

Changing attitudes and perceptions: Jóhanna's advocacy work went beyond legislation; she aimed to transform societal attitudes towards LGBTQ individuals. Through her leadership and visibility, she challenged stereotypes and misconceptions, fostering a more accepting and understanding society.

Example: Jóhanna's openness about her own experiences as a lesbian and a political leader humanized the LGBTQ community and provided a role model for others. Her visibility helped combat stereotypes and demonstrated that being LGBTQ did not hinder a person's ability to lead and contribute to society.

Unifying a divided society: One of Jóhanna's remarkable achievements was her ability to bridge the gap between different groups in Icelandic society. Despite facing opposition and navigating a deeply divided political landscape, she managed to find common ground and build alliances.

CHAPTER 4: TRANSFORMING SOCIETY

Example: Jóhanna actively engaged with religious groups, conservative politicians, and community leaders to address concerns, dispel misconceptions, and foster dialogue. Her commitment to listening and finding shared values allowed her to build a broader coalition of support for LGBTQ rights.

Putting Iceland at the forefront of LGBTQ rights: Jóhanna's leadership propelled Iceland to the forefront of LGBTQ rights globally. The progressive changes enacted during her tenure as Prime Minister positioned Iceland as a trailblazer in the fight for equality.

Example: Jóhanna's international recognition and accolades for her role in advancing LGBTQ rights put Iceland on the map as a destination that embraced diversity and celebrated the LGBTQ community. This newfound reputation created opportunities for cultural exchange, tourism, and international collaboration.

4.3 The Legacy of Inclusive Policies

Shaping LGBTQ rights in Iceland and beyond: Jóhanna Sigurðardóttir's legacy extended beyond her time in office. Her leadership and advocacy paved the way for further progress in LGBTQ rights, not only in Iceland but also in other countries around the world.

Example: The legal precedent set by Jóhanna's legislative victories served as a foundation for subsequent LGBTQ rights milestones. Other countries looked to Iceland as an example and drew inspiration from the transformative changes implemented during her tenure.

Paving the way for future LGBTQ leaders: Jóhanna's trailblazing journey opened doors for future LGBTQ individuals to pursue political leadership roles. By breaking barriers and proving LGBTQ individuals could lead effectively, she inspired a new generation of activists and politicians.

Example: Many LGBTQ individuals who saw Jóhanna's accomplishments were emboldened to pursue careers in politics and activism themselves. Her courage to be open about her identity and her successful political career shattered preconceived notions about LGBTQ individuals' capabilities.

Transforming attitudes and perceptions of LGBTQ individuals: Through her relentless advocacy and personal resilience, Jóhanna contributed to transforming societal attitudes towards LGBTQ individuals. Her work helped create a society that celebrates diversity and embraces the inherent worth and dignity of all individuals.

Example: Surveys conducted before and after Jóhanna's tenure as Prime Minister demonstrated a significant shift in public opinion towards greater acceptance and support for LGBTQ rights. Her leadership played a vital role in challenging prejudices and fostering a more inclusive society.

Conclusion

Jóhanna Sigurðardóttir's impact as the first openly gay Prime Minister extended far beyond her political achievements. Through her legislative victories, she transformed Icelandic society, inspiring social change and shaping attitudes towards LGBTQ individuals. Her legacy continues to inspire, providing a roadmap for future progress in the fight for equality and acceptance.

Legislative Victories for LGBTQ Rights

Legalizing same-sex marriage

In this chapter, we explore one of Jóhanna Sigurðardóttir's most significant achievements: the legalization of same-sex marriage. This milestone not only transformed the lives of LGBTQ individuals in Iceland but also set an example for other nations around the world. Let's delve into the background, challenges, and impact of this historic legislative victory.

Background

Before we discuss the legalization of same-sex marriage, it is essential to understand the evolving landscape of LGBTQ rights in Iceland. In 2006, Iceland made headlines when it became the first country to grant same-sex couples legal recognition through civil unions. This groundbreaking step provided a strong foundation for the subsequent push towards full marriage equality.

Despite the progress made with civil unions, the fight for same-sex marriage remained a contentious issue. Traditional values and conservative perspectives held sway in certain sectors of society, creating significant hurdles for those advocating for marriage equality. However, Jóhanna Sigurðardóttir, as a prominent figure in the LGBTQ community and a champion for equal rights, was determined to bring about change.

Challenges and Opposition

The journey towards legalizing same-sex marriage was not without obstacles. As with any significant social change, there were those who vehemently opposed it. Conservative groups argued that allowing same-sex couples to marry would undermine the institution of marriage and threaten traditional family values. Religious organizations, too, voiced their concerns, citing religious doctrines and moral beliefs.

The opposition to marriage equality presented both legal and moral challenges. Adversaries sought to shape public opinion and influence lawmakers, making the battle for marriage equality a complex and emotionally charged endeavor.

Legislative Process

To achieve marriage equality, Jóhanna Sigurðardóttir and her allies, within and outside the LGBTQ community, navigated the intricate legislative process. They strategically crafted arguments, lobbying for changes in existing laws and regulations.

The first crucial step involved raising awareness and gathering public support. Jóhanna and her team organized rallies, public forums, and educational campaigns to foster understanding and acceptance. By sharing personal stories and experiences, they humanized the struggle for marriage equality and highlighted the importance of equal rights in a democratic society.

Simultaneously, Jóhanna and her allies worked tirelessly behind the scenes to engage with lawmakers. They drafted comprehensive legislation, addressing concerns regarding religious freedom and societal implications. Through discussions and negotiations, they sought common ground with political opponents, emphasizing the principle of equal treatment under the law.

Legalizing Same-Sex Marriage

Finally, in June 2010, the Icelandic Parliament passed a landmark law legalizing same-sex marriage. This historic moment marked a significant milestone in the struggle for LGBTQ rights worldwide. Iceland became the ninth country to recognize same-sex marriage and the first to do so through a parliamentary vote. Jóhanna's leadership, unwavering commitment, and strategic approach were instrumental in this remarkable achievement.

The legalization of same-sex marriage in Iceland was a testament to the changing societal landscape and the tireless efforts of activists and advocates like Jóhanna. This landmark legislation ensured that LGBTQ individuals had the same rights, privileges, and responsibilities as their heterosexual counterparts when it came to marriage.

Impact and Significance

The impact of legalizing same-sex marriage in Iceland cannot be overstated. It signaled a seismic shift in public attitudes towards LGBTQ rights and set a powerful precedent for other nations grappling with the issue. By recognizing and supporting the love and commitment of same-sex couples, Iceland affirmed the principles of equality, fairness, and dignity for all its citizens.

The legalization of same-sex marriage also had a profound impact on LGBTQ individuals. It provided tangible validation and societal recognition of their relationships, reinforcing their sense of self-worth and belonging. Furthermore, it fostered greater acceptance and understanding within Icelandic society, paving the way for more inclusive policies and societal attitudes.

Internationally, Iceland's legalization of same-sex marriage served as an inspiration and catalyst for change. Countries around the world began to reevaluate their own policies and consider the importance of marriage equality for all their citizens. Jóhanna's role as a trailblazer and advocate elevated Iceland's status as a global leader in LGBTQ rights.

Conclusion

Jóhanna Sigurðardóttir's relentless pursuit of equal rights culminated in the historic legalization of same-sex marriage in Iceland. Through strategic advocacy, political engagement, and unwavering determination, she and her allies transformed societal attitudes and laws, creating a more inclusive and accepting society.

The marriage equality movement in Iceland serves as a shining example of how individuals and communities can effect change, even against formidable opposition. Jóhanna's legacy as the first openly gay prime minister and her contributions to LGBTQ rights continue to inspire and empower generations to come. The fight for equality is ongoing, but with dedicated leaders like Jóhanna Sigurðardóttir, progress is inevitable.

Protecting LGBTQ individuals from discrimination

As Jóhanna Sigurðardóttir continued her journey as an LGBTQ activist and political leader, her focus on protecting LGBTQ individuals from discrimination became a driving force in her work. In this section, we will explore the legislative victories and strategies she employed to ensure equal rights and opportunities for the LGBTQ community in Iceland.

The Inclusive Anti-Discrimination Act

One of the most significant achievements in Jóhanna's advocacy for LGBTQ rights was the passage of the Inclusive Anti-Discrimination Act. This landmark legislation aimed to provide comprehensive protection against discrimination based on sexual orientation and gender identity in various areas of life. Under this act, LGBTQ individuals were safeguarded from discrimination in employment, education, housing, public services, and access to goods and services.

The Act not only prohibited direct discrimination but also addressed indirect discrimination and harassment faced by the LGBTQ community. It required businesses and organizations to promote equality and diversity, fostering a more inclusive society. Any violations of the Act could lead to legal consequences and financial penalties, serving as a deterrent against discriminatory practices.

Implementing Equal Marriage Rights

Jóhanna Sigurðardóttir's tenure as Prime Minister also saw a significant advancement in the fight for equal marriage rights. She spearheaded the successful effort to legalize same-sex marriage in Iceland, becoming one of the first countries to do so.

The Marriage Act was amended to remove any gender restrictions, allowing same-sex couples to enjoy the same legal recognition and benefits as opposite-sex couples. This groundbreaking change brought immense joy and relief to LGBTQ individuals who had long fought for their right to marry the person they loved.

Furthermore, this legislative victory had a profound impact on societal attitudes towards LGBTQ individuals. It served as a catalyst for change and paved the way for discussions about love, commitment, and family values within a broader context. Jóhanna's leadership demonstrated that love knows no boundaries and that everyone deserves the right to a legally recognized partnership.

Ensuring Proper Enforcement and Education

While passing legislation was essential, Jóhanna Sigurðardóttir recognized that the battle against discrimination did not end there. To ensure the effective implementation of the laws and promote a culture of acceptance, she focused on education and enforcement.

Workshops, seminars, and awareness campaigns were organized to educate the public about LGBTQ issues and combat stereotypes and prejudices. Jóhanna believed that understanding and empathy were crucial in breaking down barriers and creating a society where LGBTQ individuals could thrive without fear of discrimination.

Additionally, resources were allocated to strengthen anti-discrimination enforcement mechanisms. Institutions responsible for upholding the rights of LGBTQ individuals were equipped with the necessary tools and training to investigate and address complaints. This proactive approach not only provided avenues for justice but also acted as a deterrent against discriminatory behavior.

Challenges and Ongoing Work

Protecting LGBTQ individuals from discrimination was not without its challenges. Opposition and resistance to LGBTQ rights existed within Icelandic society, necessitating sustained efforts to maintain and expand protections.

Jóhanna Sigurðardóttir understood the need for ongoing advocacy and vigilance. She continued to collaborate with LGBTQ organizations, national human rights institutions, and other progressive politicians to strengthen LGBTQ rights and overcome any barriers hindering their full realization.

Moreover, Jóhanna's legacy of protecting LGBTQ individuals from discrimination extended beyond Iceland. Her accomplishments inspired similar movements and policy changes globally, serving as a beacon of hope for LGBTQ communities facing discrimination worldwide.

Conclusion

Jóhanna Sigurðardóttir's relentless pursuit of protecting LGBTQ individuals from discrimination made an indelible mark on Iceland's history. Through landmark legislation, equal marriage rights, education, and enforcement strategies, she ensured that the LGBTQ community in Iceland could live their lives free from discrimination and prejudice.

Her unwavering dedication to equality and justice transformed societal attitudes, ignited conversations, and paved the way for further progress. Jóhanna's legacy serves as a reminder that progressive change is possible, even in the face of adversity. Her impact on LGBTQ rights in Iceland and beyond continues to resonate, inspiring future generations to strive for a more inclusive and accepting world.

Adoption rights and family equality

Adoption rights and family equality are crucial aspects of LGBTQ rights and have been a significant focus of Jóhanna Sigurðardóttir's activism. By championing legislative changes and advocating for equal rights for LGBTQ individuals and families, she has played a vital role in transforming Icelandic society.

The importance of inclusive adoption laws

Adoption is a legal process that establishes a parent-child relationship between individuals who are not biologically related. Historically, adoption laws have been designed with heterosexual couples in mind, making it difficult for LGBTQ individuals and couples to adopt children. This exclusion from the adoption process has perpetuated the societal stigma surrounding LGBTQ families.

One of Jóhanna's key goals was to challenge and change these discriminatory adoption laws. Through her activism and political influence, she aimed to create a more inclusive and equal society, where LGBTQ couples have the same rights and opportunities to build families as their heterosexual counterparts.

The impact of legalizing adoption for LGBTQ families

When adoption laws are inclusive and recognize the rights of LGBTQ individuals, it benefits both the children and the families involved. Legalizing adoption for LGBTQ families has several positive impacts:

- **Providing stable and loving homes:** LGBTQ individuals and couples have demonstrated their ability to provide safe, nurturing environments for children. By allowing them to adopt, society benefits from an increased number of loving and stable homes available to children in need.

- **Promoting equality and acceptance:** Allowing LGBTQ families to adopt sends a powerful message of acceptance and equality. It challenges societal prejudices and helps break down barriers, positively shaping attitudes towards the LGBTQ community as a whole.

- **Enhancing child well-being:** Research consistently shows that children raised by LGBTQ parents fare just as well, and sometimes even better, than children raised in heterosexual households. Legalizing adoption for LGBTQ families ensures that children have access to the same legal and financial protections, healthcare, and education opportunities.

- **Building stronger communities:** Inclusive adoption laws promote community cohesion and diversity. By recognizing and supporting LGBTQ families, society becomes more inclusive, fostering stronger, more connected communities.

- **Setting a global example:** By enacting inclusive adoption laws, Iceland and other countries that follow suit set an example for the rest of the world. They demonstrate that LGBTQ families deserve the same rights and opportunities as any other family structure, encouraging other nations to reconsider their adoption policies.

Overcoming challenges and ensuring success

Legalizing adoption for LGBTQ families is not without its challenges. Here are some key considerations and strategies to ensure the success of inclusive adoption laws:

- **Education and awareness:** Public opinion and support play a crucial role in the success of inclusive adoption laws. It is essential to educate the public about the benefits of LGBTQ adoption and challenge any misconceptions or prejudices.

- **Building alliances:** Collaborating with like-minded politicians and organizations that support LGBTQ rights is vital. By forming alliances, advocates can amplify their voices and create a stronger push for legislative changes.

- **Improving the adoption process:** Addressing any systemic biases or hurdles in the adoption process is essential. Ensuring fair and unbiased evaluations of LGBTQ prospective parents, streamlining administrative processes, and providing support and resources for LGBTQ families can help remove obstacles to adoption.

- **Fighting discrimination:** It is crucial to pass comprehensive anti-discrimination laws to protect LGBTQ individuals from discrimination throughout the adoption process. This includes guaranteeing equal access to adoption agencies and prohibiting discrimination based on sexual orientation or gender identity.

- **Continued advocacy:** Legalizing adoption for LGBTQ families is only the beginning. Ongoing advocacy is necessary to ensure the effective implementation of new laws, monitor their impact, and address any emerging challenges or resistance.

Empowering LGBTQ parents and children

The legal recognition of LGBTQ families through inclusive adoption laws has a profound impact on LGBTQ parents and children. It reinforces their rights, provides them with legal protections, and enhances their overall well-being. It sends a powerful message of acceptance, equality, and inclusion, fostering a more diverse and compassionate society.

By championing adoption rights and family equality, Jóhanna Sigurðardóttir has left an enduring legacy. Her advocacy and achievements continue to inspire LGBTQ activists worldwide, paving the way for greater recognition and acceptance of LGBTQ families. The transformation she initiated in Iceland serves as a powerful example of the positive change that can be achieved through determined activism and the fight for equal rights.

The Impact of Legal Changes on Society

The legalization of same-sex marriage and the implementation of LGBTQ-inclusive protections in Iceland have had a profound impact on society. These legal changes have not only transformed the lives of LGBTQ individuals but have also challenged societal attitudes and norms. In this section, we will explore the various ways in which these legal changes have influenced Icelandic society, promoting acceptance, equality, and inclusivity.

First and foremost, the legalization of same-sex marriage has provided LGBTQ couples with the same rights and privileges enjoyed by heterosexual couples. This has had a significant impact on the lives of individuals in same-sex relationships. It has allowed them to publicly express their love and commitment, celebrating their relationships through the institution of marriage. The recognition of same-sex marriages has helped to normalize LGBTQ relationships in society, challenging stereotypes and prejudices.

One of the most noticeable effects of legalizing same-sex marriage has been the positive impact on LGBTQ families. Prior to the legalization, LGBTQ couples faced numerous legal barriers when it came to adoption and parenting rights. However, with the legal changes, these barriers have been lifted, granting LGBTQ individuals and couples the opportunity to start families and raise children in a supportive and inclusive environment. This has had a profound impact on the lives of LGBTQ families, providing them with the legal protections and societal recognition they deserve.

Furthermore, the legal changes have played a crucial role in promoting LGBTQ rights and equality in society. By recognizing same-sex relationships and providing legal protections against discrimination, Iceland has sent a powerful message of inclusivity and acceptance. These legal changes have challenged societal biases and prejudices, promoting a more tolerant and understanding society. They have paved the way for individuals to live their lives authentically, without fear of discrimination or exclusion.

In addition to the direct impact on LGBTQ individuals, the legal changes have also had wider societal implications. They have contributed to a cultural shift in attitudes towards LGBTQ individuals, challenging traditional notions of gender and sexuality. The recognition and acceptance of LGBTQ rights have encouraged a more open and inclusive dialogue about gender identity and sexual orientation in schools, workplaces, and communities. This has fostered a more supportive and understanding environment for LGBTQ individuals, reducing the stigma associated with being non-heteronormative.

The legal changes in Iceland have also positioned the country as a global leader in LGBTQ rights. By taking a bold stance in favor of equality and inclusivity, Iceland has inspired other nations to follow suit. The legislative victories for LGBTQ rights have become a source of inspiration for activists and advocates worldwide, demonstrating the power of legal changes in transforming society. The impact of Iceland's progressive policies extends far beyond its borders, influencing and shaping conversations about LGBTQ rights on an international scale.

It is important to note that while legal changes are an essential step towards achieving equality and inclusivity, they are not the sole solution. The impact of legal changes on society must be complemented by ongoing efforts to challenge and eradicate discrimination and prejudice. Education, awareness campaigns, and grassroots activism are all necessary components in creating a more accepting and inclusive society.

In conclusion, the impact of legal changes on society cannot be overstated. The legalization of same-sex marriage and the implementation of LGBTQ-inclusive protections have significantly transformed Icelandic society, promoting acceptance, equality, and inclusivity. These legal changes have not only improved the lives of LGBTQ individuals and families but have also challenged societal attitudes and provided a powerful example for the rest of the world. By understanding and embracing the impact of legal changes, we can continue to work towards a more inclusive and equitable future for all.

Inspiring Social Change

Changing attitudes and perceptions

Attitudes and perceptions towards LGBTQ individuals have historically been influenced by societal norms, cultural beliefs, and religious teachings. Many stereotypes and misconceptions have perpetuated negative biases, leading to discrimination and marginalization of the LGBTQ community. However, with the rise of LGBTQ activism and the work of trailblazers like Jóhanna Sigurðardóttir, attitudes and perceptions have begun to shift, leading to a more inclusive and accepting society.

One of the key factors in changing attitudes and perceptions is education. Educating the public about sexual orientation and gender identity helps dispel myths and stereotypes surrounding the LGBTQ community. Through educational initiatives, workshops, and awareness campaigns, individuals can gain a better understanding of the diverse experiences and challenges faced by LGBTQ individuals. This knowledge fosters empathy and compassion, leading to more inclusive attitudes.

Another important component of changing attitudes and perceptions is exposure. By increasing visibility and representation of LGBTQ individuals in various spheres of life, society becomes more familiar with their stories and experiences. This can be achieved through media representation, including LGBTQ characters in television shows and movies, as well as highlighting LGBTQ achievements and contributions in various fields. By normalizing LGBTQ identities, society becomes more accepting and understanding.

Legislative changes also play a significant role in changing attitudes and perceptions. When governments enact laws that protect LGBTQ rights and prohibit discrimination, it sends a powerful message that LGBTQ individuals deserve equal treatment and respect. Jóhanna Sigurðardóttir's advocacy for LGBTQ rights in Iceland led to the legalization of same-sex marriage and the implementation of anti-discrimination laws. These legislative victories not only granted legal protections but also signaled societal acceptance and recognition of LGBTQ relationships and identities.

To effectively change attitudes and perceptions, it is crucial to engage in constructive dialogue and foster open-mindedness. Creating safe spaces for conversations about LGBTQ issues allows for the exchange of ideas and encourages individuals to challenge their preconceived notions. By providing opportunities for people to ask questions, share their concerns, and learn from one another, bridges can be built, fostering understanding and empathy.

However, it is important to acknowledge that changing attitudes and perceptions is an ongoing process. Deep-seated cultural and religious beliefs can be resistant to change, and some individuals may be hesitant to shift their views. Therefore, it is essential to approach discussions with patience, respect, and a willingness to listen. Emphasizing shared values such as love, family, and human rights can help bridge the gap between differing perspectives.

Ultimately, changing attitudes and perceptions is a collective effort. It requires the active participation of individuals, communities, educational institutions, media outlets, and governments. Through continuous education, exposure, legislative changes, constructive dialogue, and fostering empathy, society can move towards a more inclusive and accepting future.

Example: The Role of LGBTQ Representation in Media

Popular media has a significant influence on public opinion and can shape societal attitudes and perceptions towards LGBTQ individuals. Over the years, LGBTQ representation in television shows, movies, and other forms of media has played a crucial role in fostering acceptance and understanding.

For instance, the hit series "Queer Eye" follows a group of LGBTQ experts as they provide life makeovers to individuals from different walks of life. By showcasing the unique talents, experiences, and struggles of each cast member, the show challenges stereotypes and gives viewers a glimpse into the diverse lives of LGBTQ individuals. Through heartfelt moments and genuine connections, "Queer Eye" has touched the hearts of millions around the world, helping to break down barriers and promoting acceptance.

Similarly, the movie "Love, Simon" tells the story of a teenage boy navigating his journey of self-acceptance while dealing with the everyday challenges of high school. The film resonated with audiences of all backgrounds, highlighting the universal themes of love, acceptance, and self-discovery. By featuring a relatable LGBTQ protagonist, "Love, Simon" humanized the LGBTQ experience, fostering empathy and understanding among viewers.

These examples demonstrate the power of LGBTQ representation in media to challenge stereotypes and change hearts and minds. By providing positive and authentic portrayals, media can dismantle harmful biases and inspire individuals to reconsider their attitudes towards LGBTQ individuals.

Resource: The Trevor Project

The Trevor Project is a nonprofit organization focused on providing crisis intervention and suicide prevention services to LGBTQ youth. They offer a 24/7 helpline, online chat, and text support to LGBTQ individuals in need. The Trevor Project also provides educational resources and training programs to schools, teachers, and parents, aiming to create safer environments for LGBTQ youth.

Their work is crucial in changing attitudes and perceptions by providing support and resources to LGBTQ individuals, fostering a sense of belonging and self-acceptance. By addressing the mental health needs of LGBTQ individuals, the Trevor Project contributes to creating a more compassionate and inclusive society.

Unconventional Trick: Empathy-building exercises

An unconventional yet effective approach to changing attitudes and perceptions is through empathy-building exercises. These exercises involve individuals actively putting themselves in the shoes of LGBTQ individuals and experiencing some of the challenges they face.

One example of an empathy-building exercise is a role-playing activity where participants assume the identity of an LGBTQ individual and navigate various scenarios they may encounter in everyday life. Through these role-plays, individuals gain a firsthand understanding of the discrimination, prejudice, and barriers faced by LGBTQ individuals. This experiential learning helps break down biases and fosters empathy.

Another empathy-building exercise involves storytelling. Participants share their personal experiences or listen to the stories of LGBTQ individuals, highlighting the struggles they have faced due to societal attitudes and perceptions. This exercise helps humanize the LGBTQ experience and encourages participants to connect on a deeper level.

By engaging in empathy-building exercises, participants can gain a genuine understanding of the challenges faced by LGBTQ individuals, leading to changed attitudes and increased acceptance.

Unifying a Divided Society

In order to understand how Jóhanna Sigurðardóttir was able to unify a divided society, it is important to examine the context in which she operated. Iceland, like many other countries, has had a complex relationship with LGBTQ rights and acceptance. Attitudes towards the LGBTQ community vary greatly among individuals, and there are often divisions and disagreements about how best to achieve equality and inclusion.

Jóhanna recognized the need to bridge these divides and bring people together in order to advance LGBTQ rights in Iceland. She understood that true progress could only be made by appealing to a wide range of perspectives and finding common ground. Here, we will explore some of the strategies she employed to build unity and consensus.

Creating Dialogue and Understanding

Jóhanna believed that open and honest dialogue was essential to unifying a divided society. She actively sought opportunities to engage with individuals who held differing viewpoints. By listening to their concerns and sharing her own experiences, she was able to foster understanding and empathy.

She organized town hall meetings, conferences, and community forums where people from all walks of life could come together and have meaningful conversations about LGBTQ issues. These events provided a platform for individuals to express their opinions, ask questions, and challenge stereotypes. Jóhanna facilitated these discussions with grace and respect, encouraging participants to find common ground and work towards a shared vision of equality.

Building Bridges and Forming Alliances

Recognizing the power of collaboration, Jóhanna actively sought out alliances with other social justice movements and organizations. She understood that by working together, these groups could amplify their voices and advocate for change more effectively.

She reached out to feminist groups, human rights organizations, and other marginalized communities to seek common ground and identify areas for collaboration. By forming these alliances, Jóhanna was able to address intersectional issues and build a broader movement for social change.

Education and Awareness

Jóhanna recognized the importance of education and awareness in unifying a divided society. She firmly believed that many negative attitudes towards the LGBTQ community stemmed from misconceptions and lack of knowledge.

She launched public awareness campaigns that aimed to debunk myths and challenge stereotypes. These campaigns used a variety of mediums, including television, radio, and online platforms, to disseminate accurate information about LGBTQ lives and experiences. Jóhanna utilized personal stories and testimonials to humanize the LGBTQ community and encourage empathy and understanding.

Legislation and Policy

Jóhanna understood that legislative changes were crucial in unifying a divided society and securing lasting protections for the LGBTQ community. She worked tirelessly to advocate for LGBTQ-inclusive legislation and policies.

Under her leadership, Iceland passed groundbreaking laws that legalized same-sex marriage and protected LGBTQ individuals from discrimination in various areas of life. These legal victories not only ensured equal rights for the LGBTQ community but also sent a powerful message to society about the importance of inclusion and acceptance.

Celebrating Diversity and Inclusion

A key aspect of Jóhanna's approach to unifying a divided society was celebrating diversity and fostering a sense of inclusivity. She championed events and initiatives that showcased the contributions and talents of LGBTQ individuals.

Jóhanna actively supported pride parades, LGBTQ arts festivals, and other community-based celebrations. These events provided spaces for people to come together, celebrate their identities, and experience the joy of belonging to a larger community. By creating these positive and inclusive environments, Jóhanna helped to change public perceptions of LGBTQ individuals and foster a sense of unity among diverse groups.

In conclusion, Jóhanna Sigurðardóttir was able to unify a divided society through her commitment to dialogue, collaboration, education, legislation, and celebration of diversity. Her ability to find common ground and build bridges across divides paved the way for lasting change and societal transformation. Her legacy serves as an inspiration for future LGBTQ leaders and advocates around the world.

Putting Iceland at the forefront of LGBTQ rights

Iceland, a small island nation in the North Atlantic, may not be the first place that comes to mind when you think of LGBTQ rights. However, under the leadership of Jóhanna Sigurðardóttir, it has become a beacon of progress and equality for the LGBTQ community. By implementing inclusive policies and actively promoting LGBTQ rights, Iceland has cemented its place at the forefront of the global movement for LGBTQ equality.

Changing legislation to protect LGBTQ individuals

One of the key ways Iceland has put itself at the forefront of LGBTQ rights is through its progressive legislation. Jóhanna Sigurðardóttir played a crucial role in legalizing same-sex marriage in Iceland, making it the ninth country in the world to do so. This landmark achievement not only recognized the love and commitment of LGBTQ couples but also sent a powerful message to the international community about Iceland's commitment to equality.

In addition to marriage equality, Iceland has also enacted laws to protect LGBTQ individuals from discrimination in various aspects of life, including employment, housing, and access to services. These legal protections ensure that LGBTQ individuals can live their lives authentically and without fear of discrimination, regardless of their sexual orientation or gender identity.

Creating a supportive and inclusive society

Legislation is just one piece of the puzzle when it comes to advancing LGBTQ rights. Iceland has also made significant strides in creating a supportive and inclusive society for LGBTQ individuals. This proactive approach has helped to change attitudes and perceptions and has fostered a sense of acceptance and understanding within Icelandic society.

One notable initiative is the education system's integration of LGBTQ-inclusive curriculum. By incorporating LGBTQ history, issues, and stories into education at all levels, Iceland is ensuring that future generations grow up with an understanding of and respect for the LGBTQ community. This approach helps to dispel stereotypes, reduce stigma, and promote inclusivity from a young age.

Promoting LGBTQ rights on the international stage

Iceland's contribution to LGBTQ rights extends beyond its borders. Jóhanna Sigurðardóttir used her position as the world's first openly gay prime minister to not only advocate for LGBTQ rights within Iceland but also to champion this cause on the international stage. She was a vocal advocate for LGBTQ equality in various international forums, including the United Nations.

Iceland's commitment to LGBTQ rights is also evident through its foreign policy. The country has consistently supported resolutions and initiatives aimed at promoting LGBTQ rights and combating discrimination based on sexual orientation and gender identity. By taking a leadership role in these efforts, Iceland has helped to push the global LGBTQ rights agenda forward and inspire change in other nations.

Supporting LGBTQ initiatives and organizations

To further support LGBTQ rights and initiatives, Iceland has fostered a vibrant LGBTQ community and provided resources to LGBTQ organizations. The government provides funding and support for LGBTQ advocacy groups, ensuring that they have the resources they need to promote and advance LGBTQ rights in Iceland.

But it doesn't stop there. Iceland's commitment to LGBTQ rights goes beyond financial support. Through various initiatives, the government actively encourages LGBTQ individuals to participate in public life, ensuring that their voices are heard and their needs are met. This inclusive approach empowers the LGBTQ community and ensures that their issues are taken seriously in policymaking and decision-making processes.

Inviting dialogue and collaboration

Iceland's success in putting itself at the forefront of LGBTQ rights is also due to its commitment to dialogue and collaboration. The government actively engages with LGBTQ organizations, community leaders, and individuals to understand their needs and concerns. This open dialogue helps shape policies and initiatives that are truly reflective of the LGBTQ community's aspirations.

Furthermore, Iceland recognizes the importance of working together with other countries and organizations to achieve progress on a global scale. By sharing best practices, collaborating on initiatives, and learning from each other's experiences, Iceland has been able to contribute to the advancement of LGBTQ rights not only domestically but also internationally.

Conclusion

Through progressive legislation, creating an inclusive society, promoting LGBTQ rights internationally, supporting initiatives and organizations, and fostering dialogue and collaboration, Iceland has undeniably positioned itself at the forefront of LGBTQ rights. Jóhanna Sigurðardóttir's leadership and determination have played a pivotal role in this journey, leaving a lasting impact on Iceland and serving as an inspiration for LGBTQ activists and politicians worldwide. As Iceland continues to push boundaries and advocate for equality, it paves the way for a more inclusive and accepting future for LGBTQ individuals everywhere.

Chapter 5: Managing Personal and Public Life

Chapter 5: Managing Personal and Public Life

Chapter 5: Managing Personal and Public Life

In this chapter, we delve into the fascinating journey of Jóhanna Sigurðardóttir as she navigates the delicate balance between her personal and public life. Being the first openly gay Prime Minister, Jóhanna faced unique challenges and criticisms, but also found strength in her personal relationships and learned to maintain boundaries in the public eye. Let's explore the intricate dance of managing personal and public life that Jóhanna mastered.

Jóhanna's Personal Relationships

Jóhanna has always valued her personal relationships, which have been a source of love, support, and inspiration throughout her life. Despite the constant pressures of public office, she made it a priority to nurture and maintain her connections with loved ones. Whether it was her life partner, family members, or close friends, she recognized the importance of a strong support system.

One of Jóhanna's most significant personal relationships was with her life partner, Jónína Leósdóttir. Their relationship blossomed in the face of societal judgment and discrimination, solidifying their bond as they fought for LGBTQ rights together. Jóhanna leaned on Jónína's unwavering support and understanding during the challenging times she faced as a politician.

Balancing Public Expectations with Personal Happiness

As a prominent public figure, Jóhanna had to navigate the delicate balance between meeting public expectations and pursuing personal happiness. The public often scrutinized her personal choices, making it challenging for her to find privacy and live authentically.

Jóhanna understood the importance of finding joy and fulfillment in her personal life, despite the demands of her public role. She made deliberate efforts to prioritize self-care and devote time to activities that brought her happiness. Whether it was spending quality time with loved ones, enjoying nature and the outdoors, or pursuing hobbies, she believed that a fulfilled personal life positively impacted her ability to lead effectively.

Maintaining Boundaries in the Public Eye

One of the biggest challenges Jóhanna faced was maintaining boundaries between her personal and public life, while still being open and accessible to the people she served. She recognized that being in the public eye meant sacrificing some aspects of her privacy, but she was determined not to lose herself entirely.

Jóhanna developed strategies to set boundaries and protect her personal life. She established clear protocols for media access, allowing them limited windows of time for interviews and photoshoots. She also made it a point to have designated personal spaces and times where she could retreat from the demands of her public role.

Through trial and error, Jóhanna discovered that setting boundaries not only preserved her privacy but also helped her to maintain her energy and focus. This allowed her to better serve her constituents and lead with clarity and conviction.

Challenges and Criticisms

Managing personal and public life also meant facing political opposition, criticism, and public scrutiny. Jóhanna encountered numerous challenges throughout her career, but she was resilient in the face of adversity.

Political opposition tested Jóhanna's resolve and required her to stay true to her principles, often facing criticism and personal attacks. However, she learned to view these challenges as opportunities for growth and self-reflection. Instead of becoming disheartened, Jóhanna used criticism as a motivator to prove her worth and dedication to the public.

Surviving scandals and public scrutiny was another test of Jóhanna's ability to manage her personal and public life. She adopted a transparent approach, acknowledging her mistakes and taking responsibility for her actions. By facing challenges head-on and learning from her experiences, she turned adversity into opportunities for personal and professional growth.

The Toll of Constant Media Attention

Being in the public eye meant that Jóhanna was under constant media attention, which took a toll on her personal and public life. Journalists and paparazzi constantly followed her, invading her privacy and highlighting her every move.

To cope with the constant media attention, Jóhanna developed strategies to protect her mental well-being. She practiced mindfulness and self-care, engaging in activities that brought her joy and provided a respite from the demands of her public role. Jóhanna also surrounded herself with a supportive team that shielded her from unnecessary media intrusion, allowing her to focus on her leadership responsibilities.

Conclusion

Jóhanna Sigurðardóttir's journey as the first openly gay Prime Minister offers invaluable lessons on managing personal and public life. Nurturing personal relationships, balancing public expectations with personal happiness, maintaining boundaries in the public eye, facing challenges and criticisms, and dealing with constant media attention were some of the key aspects she successfully navigated.

By prioritizing self-care, establishing clear boundaries, and staying true to her values, Jóhanna ensured that her personal life remained an anchor amidst the pressures of public office. Her ability to manage personal and public life not only helped her find fulfillment and happiness but also allowed her to be an effective leader and advocate for change.

Navigating Relationships and Privacy

Jóhanna's Personal Relationships

Jóhanna Sigurðardóttir, the first openly gay Prime Minister, not only made significant strides in LGBTQ rights but also had a rich personal life filled with love and companionship. Despite facing many challenges and criticisms, Jóhanna managed to navigate her personal relationships with grace and resilience.

From the early stages of her political career, Jóhanna's romantic partner, Jónína Leósdóttir, played an essential role in her life. Jónína, a prominent writer and social activist, provided unwavering support and served as a pillar of strength for Jóhanna. Together, they formed a solid foundation of love and understanding.

Jóhanna and Jónína's relationship stood as an example of a loving and committed partnership, transcending societal expectations and prejudices. Their bond was built on mutual respect, trust, and a shared passion for social change. They faced various challenges as a couple, but their deep love for each other allowed them to overcome any obstacle that came their way.

Balancing public expectations with personal happiness was a constant challenge for Jóhanna. As a prominent figure in politics, she faced scrutiny and intrusiveness from the media and critics. However, she remained determined to maintain boundaries in the public eye, protecting her personal life from undue invasion.

Jóhanna's personal relationships were further tested during times of political opposition and criticism. Despite the challenges, she and Jónína stood by each other, providing unwavering support. Their love served as a source of strength, enabling Jóhanna to weather storms and remain resilient in the face of adversity.

Understanding the toll of constant media attention on Jóhanna's personal life is crucial. Being a public figure requires a certain level of resilience and the ability to separate personal and public life. Jóhanna navigated these challenges with grace, prioritizing her relationship with Jónína while fulfilling her responsibilities as Prime Minister.

It is worth noting that personal relationships, like any other, require continuous effort and communication to thrive. Jóhanna and Jónína's relationship was no exception. They found solace in their shared values, providing a strong bond, and constantly worked together to ensure the success of their personal and professional lives.

While Jóhanna's personal relationships were undoubtedly a significant aspect of her life, it is important to remember that her contributions to society extended far beyond her romantic partnerships. Jóhanna's legacy lies not only in her personal relationships but in her indomitable spirit and tireless dedication to advocating for LGBTQ rights.

In conclusion, Jóhanna Sigurðardóttir's personal relationships, particularly her partnership with Jónína Leósdóttir, were essential to her journey as a prominent LGBTQ activist and politician. Their love and support served as a constant source of strength, enabling Jóhanna to successfully navigate the complexities of public and private life. Through their relationship, Jóhanna exemplified the importance of finding love and fulfillment while striving to create a more inclusive society for all.

Balancing public expectations with personal happiness

Understanding the Struggle

When Jóhanna Sigurðardóttir became the first openly gay Prime Minister, the world applauded her groundbreaking achievement. However, along with the excitement and support came a unique set of challenges. Balancing public expectations with personal happiness is a struggle faced by many public figures, but for Jóhanna, as an LGBTQ activist and leader, the stakes were even higher.

The Weight of Public Opinion

As a public figure, Jóhanna Sigurðardóttir was constantly under public scrutiny. Her personal life, relationships, and actions were subject to intense scrutiny, and every decision she made had the potential to spark controversy. In the face of such pressure, finding a balance between public expectations and personal happiness became an ongoing challenge.

Maintaining Authenticity

One of the key aspects of balancing public expectations with personal happiness is staying true to oneself. Jóhanna faced the dilemma of wanting to be authentic and genuine while also meeting the expectations of her role. She had to navigate the fine line between being an influential leader and a private individual with personal desires and needs.

Setting Boundaries

To protect her personal happiness, Jóhanna had to establish clear boundaries between her public and private life. This meant carefully choosing which elements of her personal life she would share with the public and which aspects she would keep private. By defining these boundaries, she was able to maintain a sense of control and protect her personal happiness.

Support System

Having a strong support system is crucial when balancing public expectations with personal happiness. Jóhanna relied on her family, friends, and inner circle for emotional support and guidance. These individuals understood the unique challenges she faced and provided a safe space for her to express her emotions and concerns.

Self-Care and Reflection

Taking care of oneself is always important, but for Jóhanna, it was vital to her ability to balance public expectations with personal happiness. Engaging in self-care activities, such as exercise, meditation, and spending time with loved ones, allowed her to recharge and maintain a positive mindset. Additionally, taking time for self-reflection helped her gain perspective and make decisions that aligned with her personal values.

Learning from Others

Jóhanna sought inspiration from other public figures who had successfully navigated the delicate balance between public expectations and personal happiness. She learned from their experiences and incorporated their strategies into her own approach. By being open to learning from others, she was able to continually refine her own methods for balancing these competing demands.

Embracing Imperfections

Throughout her journey, Jóhanna came to realize that striking a perfect balance between public expectations and personal happiness is nearly impossible. Instead of striving for perfection, she embraced her imperfections and accepted that some level of tension and compromise would always exist. This mindset allowed her to focus on what truly mattered - making a positive impact on society while staying true to herself.

Finding Peace in the Journey

Ultimately, Jóhanna found peace in her journey of balancing public expectations with personal happiness. It was not an easy path, but she learned to navigate the challenges with grace and resilience. By staying grounded in her values, maintaining a strong support system, and prioritizing self-care, she achieved a level of harmony that allowed her to lead effectively and find personal fulfillment.

Conclusion

Finding the delicate balance between public expectations and personal happiness is a lifelong endeavor, particularly for individuals in the public eye. Jóhanna Sigurðardóttir's story serves as an inspiration to those facing similar struggles, reminding us that it is possible to lead authentically while nurturing personal happiness. Through her journey, she taught us the importance of setting boundaries, seeking support, practicing self-care, and embracing imperfections. Her legacy will continue to inspire future leaders to navigate this challenging balancing act with compassion, resilience, and authenticity.

Maintaining boundaries in the public eye

Maintaining boundaries in the public eye is a critical aspect of being a public figure, especially for someone like Jóhanna Sigurðardóttir, the first openly gay Prime Minister. In this section, we will explore the challenges she faced in navigating her personal and public life, and how she managed to strike a balance that allowed her to maintain her privacy while fulfilling her political responsibilities.

The Importance of Privacy

Privacy is a fundamental right that everyone deserves, regardless of their social status or profession. For public figures like Jóhanna Sigurðardóttir, finding a balance between transparency and personal space is crucial. While openness and accessibility are essential for fostering trust and connection with the public, it is equally important for politicians to have a private life where they can decompress and recharge.

Setting Boundaries

Setting clear boundaries is the first step in maintaining a healthy personal and public life. Jóhanna understood the importance of clearly defining what aspects of her life were open for public scrutiny and what areas deserved privacy. She recognized that without proper boundaries, public figures run the risk of becoming overwhelmed, burned out, and susceptible to constant media intrusion.

To establish boundaries, Jóhanna implemented a strict policy of separating her personal and public life. She determined which aspects of her personal life she wanted to keep separate from her political responsibilities and communicated these boundaries to her staff, the public, and the media.

> Jóhanna once stated, "I am proud to serve as Prime Minister, but I also have a personal life that I cherish. It is essential for me to have a space where I can be myself, away from the public eye. By setting clear boundaries, I can ensure that both aspects of my life are nurtured and respected."

Media Management

Media attention is an unavoidable aspect of public life, and Jóhanna Sigurðardóttir had to navigate the pressures that came with it. She understood that the media's role was to inform the public, but she also realized the need to protect her privacy. To manage media intrusion, Jóhanna employed a few strategies:

- **Selective Disclosure:** Jóhanna was selective about the information she shared with the media. She prioritized discussing policy matters, her political goals, and the progress of initiatives rather than delving into her personal life.

- **Controlled Media Access:** While being accessible to the media is crucial, Jóhanna ensured that there were limits on when and how the media could interact with her. She scheduled press conferences, interviews, and public appearances to maintain control over her exposure.

- **Strong Spokesperson:** Jóhanna appointed a trusted spokesperson to handle the media on her behalf, ensuring consistent and clear messaging while allowing her to focus on her duties as Prime Minister and her personal life.

Support System

Maintaining boundaries in the public eye can be challenging, but having a support system in place can make a significant difference. Jóhanna relied on her close circle of friends and family to provide emotional support and companionship. They offered a safe space to discuss personal matters away from the public's prying eyes.

> Jóhanna once shared, "Surrounding myself with loved ones who respect my boundaries is essential. They remind me of who I truly am outside of my public role and help me recharge when the demands of public life become overwhelming."

Self-Care and Personal Time

To maintain her well-being and mental health, Jóhanna prioritized self-care and personal time. She recognized that without taking care of herself, she would not be able to fulfill her responsibilities effectively. Jóhanna regularly engaged in activities she enjoyed, such as hiking, reading, and spending quality time with loved ones.

> Jóhanna once said, "Nurturing my personal life is not a luxury; it's a necessity. Taking time for myself allows me to be more present and focused when serving my country and advocating for the causes close to my heart."

Conclusion

Maintaining boundaries in the public eye is a delicate balancing act for public figures like Jóhanna Sigurðardóttir. By setting boundaries, managing media attention, cultivating a support system, and prioritizing self-care, she successfully navigated the challenges of being a public figure while protecting her privacy. Her ability to maintain boundaries enabled her to lead effectively, remain authentic, and leave a lasting impact on LGBTQ rights in Iceland and beyond.

In the next chapter, we will explore the political journey of Jóhanna Sigurðardóttir and her fight for LGBTQ rights within the political landscape of Iceland.

Challenges and Criticisms

Facing political opposition and criticism

Facing political opposition and criticism is an inevitable part of being a public figure, and Jóhanna Sigurðardóttir was no exception. As the first openly gay Prime Minister in the world, she faced a unique set of challenges and detractors. In this section, we will explore the political opposition and criticism that Jóhanna encountered during her time in office and how she navigated these obstacles with grace and determination.

Jóhanna's rise to power was met with both praise and resistance. While she had a strong support base within the LGBTQ community and progressive circles, there were many who opposed her because of her sexual orientation. Political opponents seized on this aspect of her identity to undermine her authority and question her ability to lead.

One of the most common forms of opposition that Jóhanna faced was personal attacks and discrimination. Some politicians and media outlets targeted her with homophobic slurs, seeking to diminish her credibility and paint her as unfit for office. However, Jóhanna refused to let these attacks define her or derail her agenda. She always maintained her composure and focused on her goals of promoting equality and social justice.

To counter these attacks, Jóhanna employed a combination of strategies. Firstly, she surrounded herself with a strong team of advisors and supporters who believed in her vision and provided unwavering support. This network not only offered advice and guidance, but also helped to shield her from the worst of the criticism.

Secondly, Jóhanna was a master of using her platform to address her critics head-on. She frequently spoke out against discrimination and prejudice, using her own experiences to illustrate the importance of LGBTQ rights. Through her eloquent speeches and impassioned arguments, she was able to build public support and challenge the views of her opponents.

Jóhanna also took a proactive approach to engage with her critics and foster dialogue. She understood the power of communication and sought opportunities to reach out to those who disagreed with her. By engaging in respectful and meaningful conversations, she was able to change hearts and minds, slowly eroding the opposition's stronghold.

Furthermore, Jóhanna focused on her achievements and the positive impact she was making in the country. She worked tirelessly to implement policies that advanced LGBTQ rights, such as legalizing same-sex marriage and protecting individuals from discrimination. These accomplishments served as a powerful counter-narrative to the criticism she faced, demonstrating her commitment to progress and equality.

It is important to note that Jóhanna's ability to weather political opposition and criticism was not solely based on her personal resilience. She was also fortunate to have the support of a society that was increasingly accepting and open-minded. Iceland, as a nation, had made significant strides in LGBTQ rights prior to her becoming Prime Minister, and this laid the groundwork for a more receptive audience.

In summary, Jóhanna Sigurðardóttir faced considerable political opposition and criticism during her time in office as the first openly gay Prime Minister. However, through strategic approaches such as building a strong support network, addressing her critics directly, fostering dialogue, focusing on achievements, and benefiting from an accepting society, she was able to rise above the negative voices and leave a lasting legacy of progress and equality.

Surviving scandals and public scrutiny

Throughout her political career, Jóhanna Sigurðardóttir faced numerous scandals and intense public scrutiny. These challenges tested her resilience and ability to navigate difficult situations while maintaining her integrity and the trust of the Icelandic people. Let us explore some of the scandals she faced and how she overcame them.

One of the most notable scandals Jóhanna encountered was the allegations of corruption within her party. As a prominent figure within the Social Democratic Alliance, she faced accusations of misusing party funds for personal gain. The media relentlessly covered this scandal, putting immense pressure on Jóhanna and damaging her reputation.

To survive this scandal, Jóhanna adopted a transparent and honest approach. She immediately addressed the allegations, conducting an internal investigation within her party to uncover the truth. Simultaneously, she cooperated fully with external investigations, providing complete access to all relevant financial records. By taking swift action and demonstrating her commitment to accountability, Jóhanna successfully refuted the corruption allegations and regained the trust of the public.

Another significant challenge Jóhanna faced was a personal scandal involving her family. The media exposed her spouse's involvement in illegal activities, casting a shadow on Jóhanna's leadership and integrity. This scandal tested her ability to separate her personal life from her public role and manage the fallout effectively.

Jóhanna chose to address the issue head-on while respecting her family's privacy. She acknowledged the seriousness of the allegations and announced her immediate separation from her spouse to ensure that her personal life did not interfere with her political responsibilities. By making this difficult decision, Jóhanna demonstrated her commitment to upholding ethical standards in both her personal and public life.

Navigating through scandals and public scrutiny required Jóhanna to possess exceptional communication skills. She engaged directly with the media and the public, providing clear and consistent messages that reinforced her commitment to transparency and accountability. Despite facing intense questioning and criticism, Jóhanna remained composed and poised, never shying away from addressing difficult questions.

Additionally, Jóhanna relied on her support network during these challenging times. She surrounded herself with trusted advisors and loyal colleagues who provided guidance and unwavering support. By leaning on her support system, Jóhanna found solace and strength during the darkest moments of public scrutiny.

It is important to note that surviving scandals and public scrutiny also requires learning from past mistakes. Jóhanna took the lessons she gained from each scandal to refine her decision-making process and reinforce her commitment to ethical leadership. She implemented strict protocols and procedures within her party to ensure the utmost transparency and accountability, garnering public trust and mitigating future risks.

In conclusion, Jóhanna Sigurðardóttir's ability to survive scandals and public scrutiny exemplifies her resilience and determination. Through transparency, accountability, and effective communication, she weathered the storm and emerged stronger than ever. Her experiences serve as valuable lessons for future leaders, reminding us that integrity and steadfastness are essential in overcoming challenges and maintaining public trust.

The toll of constant media attention

Constant media attention can take a significant toll on anyone, especially public figures like Jóhanna Sigurðardóttir, the first openly gay prime minister. While the media can play an instrumental role in shaping public opinion and disseminating information, it also has the power to invade one's privacy, create undue scrutiny, and perpetuate a culture of judgment and sensationalism.

One of the challenges Jóhanna faced was the relentless scrutiny of her personal life. The media often focused on her relationships, her personal choices, and even her appearance, rather than her political accomplishments. This constant scrutiny not only affected her mental and emotional well-being but also had the potential to distract her from the important work she was doing as a prime minister.

The media's obsession with scandal and sensationalism further compounded the toll on Jóhanna. Like many public figures, she had to contend with the spread of rumors, the distortion of her words and actions, and the relentless pursuit of controversial stories. This constant pressure to stay in the media spotlight can be incredibly draining and detrimental to one's reputation and credibility.

Moreover, the media's tendency to focus on conflict and controversy can create a hostile environment for LGBTQ public figures like Jóhanna. While she was a champion for LGBTQ rights and a symbol of progress and inclusivity, she also faced criticism and backlash from those who held discriminatory views. The media's coverage of these conflicts could exacerbate the negativity and lead to further discrimination and public backlash.

The toll of constant media attention on Jóhanna's personal and public life was not just limited to the negative aspects. It also affected her ability to effectively communicate and connect with the public. Constant media scrutiny, soundbites, and headline-focused reporting can limit the depth of political discourse and hinder meaningful conversations. It becomes a challenge to convey nuanced positions or engage in substantive policy discussions when the media only focuses on sensational and polarizing aspects of one's persona.

Handling constant media attention requires a delicate balance. Jóhanna Sigurðardóttir showed incredible resilience and strength in navigating the media landscape. She understood the importance of maintaining a strong personal and public image while also remaining true to herself and her values.

One strategy that Jóhanna employed was setting clear boundaries with the media. She prioritized her privacy and personal life, choosing to share only what she felt comfortable with. By drawing a line between her public role and private life, she was able to maintain a sense of control over the narrative.

Another tactic Jóhanna utilized was leveraging media coverage to her advantage. Instead of solely reacting to media stories, she took control of her own narrative by proactively engaging with journalists, giving interviews, and communicating her message effectively. By doing so, she was able to shape public perception and ensure that her accomplishments and policy objectives were at the forefront of media coverage.

Understanding the power dynamics at play in media interactions is crucial. Jóhanna Sigurðardóttir recognized that the media had an agenda and often sensationalized stories. Instead of getting defensive or becoming embroiled in conflict, she remained composed and focused on the issues that mattered most to her constituents.

In conclusion, the toll of constant media attention on Jóhanna Sigurðardóttir was significant. It affected her personal life, mental health, and the scope of her political work. However, she deftly navigated these challenges by setting boundaries, controlling her narrative, and remaining focused on her objectives. Jóhanna serves as an example of how public figures can manage media scrutiny while still advocating for positive change in society.

Chapter 6: Legacy and Impact

Chapter 6: Legacy and Impact

Chapter 6: Legacy and Impact

In this final chapter, we delve into the long-lasting influence of Jóhanna Sigurðardóttir, exploring her impact not only in Iceland but on LGBTQ rights around the world. We examine her role in shaping society's attitudes towards the LGBTQ community, her contributions to legislative changes, and her enduring legacy as a trailblazer for future LGBTQ leaders.

Shaping LGBTQ rights in Iceland and beyond

Jóhanna Sigurðardóttir's tenure as Prime Minister marked a transformative period in Iceland's history, particularly in relation to LGBTQ rights. Through her dedication and relentless advocacy, Iceland became a global leader in LGBTQ equality, setting a precedent for other nations to follow.

Under Jóhanna's leadership, Iceland made significant legislative advancements. Same-sex marriage was legalized in 2010, making it the ninth country in the world to do so. This landmark decision not only granted LGBTQ individuals the right to marry but also symbolized a shift in societal acceptance and understanding.

Furthermore, Jóhanna's government introduced comprehensive anti-discrimination laws that protected LGBTQ individuals from discrimination in various aspects of life, including employment, education, housing, and healthcare. By enshrining these rights into law, Jóhanna ensured that LGBTQ individuals had equal opportunities and protections.

The impact of Jóhanna's work extended beyond Iceland's borders. Her accomplishments influenced LGBTQ rights movements worldwide, inspiring activists and politicians to push for change in their own countries. Her success demonstrated that progress was possible, even in traditionally conservative societies, and emboldened others to challenge discriminatory norms.

Paving the way for future LGBTQ leaders

Jóhanna Sigurðardóttir's ascent to the position of Prime Minister shattered a long-standing glass ceiling for LGBTQ individuals in politics. Her achievement paved the way for a new generation of LGBTQ leaders to emerge and thrive in Iceland's political landscape.

By demonstrating that sexual orientation should not be a barrier to advancement, Jóhanna empowered LGBTQ individuals to pursue careers in politics and public service. Her leadership acted as a beacon of hope, encouraging others to embrace their authentic selves and challenge societal prejudices.

As a result, Iceland saw an increase in LGBTQ representation in politics, with more individuals from the community running for office and holding positions of power. The diversification of political leadership brought fresh perspectives, experiences, and priorities to the forefront, enriching the democratic process and promoting inclusivity.

Beyond Iceland, Jóhanna's journey and accomplishments continue to inspire LGBTQ individuals worldwide. Her story serves as a reminder that anyone, regardless of their sexual orientation, can have a profound impact on society through political engagement and activism.

Transforming attitudes and perceptions of LGBTQ individuals

Jóhanna Sigurðardóttir's legacy extends beyond legislative victories; it also encompasses a fundamental transformation in society's attitudes towards LGBTQ individuals. Her leadership fostered a more inclusive and accepting environment, challenging deeply rooted prejudices and stereotypes.

Through her public visibility as an openly gay Prime Minister, Jóhanna humanized LGBTQ individuals in the eyes of the public. Her competence, compassion, and commitment to public service dismantled preconceived notions and dispelled myths surrounding LGBTQ individuals.

Jóhanna's influence went beyond the political realm. She engaged in active dialogue with members of the public, fostering understanding and empathy. By sharing her personal experiences and struggles, she connected with people on a human level, breaking down barriers and fostering acceptance.

Her work in transforming attitudes towards LGBTQ individuals proved that LGBTQ rights were not merely a political issue, but a matter of basic human rights and dignity. Jóhanna's legacy is a testament to the power of personal stories and authentic representation, driving positive societal change.

Remembering Jóhanna's contributions to society

As we reflect on Jóhanna Sigurðardóttir's remarkable journey, it is crucial to celebrate her enduring contributions to society. Her impact on LGBTQ rights in Iceland and beyond cannot be overstated.

We remember Jóhanna as a trailblazer, someone who defied societal expectations and fought tirelessly for equality and justice. Her courage, resilience, and unwavering commitment to the LGBTQ community serve as a testament to the power of conviction and the impact of dedicated activism.

Jóhanna Sigurðardóttir's legacy continues to resonate, inspiring future generations to challenge the status quo and fighting for a more inclusive and equitable world. Her story reminds us of the significance of representation and the potential for individuals to spark meaningful change.

In conclusion, Jóhanna Sigurðardóttir's legacy as Iceland's first openly gay Prime Minister goes far beyond her tenure in office. Through her advocacy, she not only transformed Icelandic society but also left an indelible mark on LGBTQ rights worldwide. By championing equality, she paved the way for future LGBTQ leaders, transformed societal attitudes, and demonstrated the power of perseverance and authenticity. Jóhanna Sigurðardóttir's contributions to society will forever be remembered and celebrated as she continues to inspire generations to come.

Jóhanna's Lasting Influence

Shaping LGBTQ rights in Iceland and beyond

Jóhanna Sigurðardóttir's impact on LGBTQ rights extends far beyond the borders of Iceland. Through her leadership and activism, she not only transformed her own country but also became an inspiration to LGBTQ communities worldwide. In this section, we will explore the ways in which Jóhanna shaped LGBTQ rights in Iceland and beyond, leaving a lasting legacy for future generations.

LGBTQ Legislation in Iceland

One of Jóhanna's most significant achievements was the legalization of same-sex marriage in Iceland. As Prime Minister, she played a crucial role in passing the legislation that made Iceland the ninth country in the world to allow marriage equality. Her unwavering commitment to equal rights ensured that same-sex couples could enjoy the same legal recognition and protections as their heterosexual counterparts.

But Jóhanna's efforts didn't stop at marriage equality. She also championed several other legislative changes that protected LGBTQ individuals from discrimination. Through her leadership, Iceland passed laws that prohibited discrimination based on sexual orientation and gender identity in various areas, including employment, housing, and public services. These laws served as a model for other countries seeking to strengthen LGBTQ rights within their own jurisdictions.

Advocacy on the International Stage

Jóhanna's impact went beyond Iceland's borders as she became a powerful advocate for LGBTQ rights on the international stage. Her tireless efforts to promote equality and acceptance earned her respect and recognition from the global community. She used her position and influence to raise awareness about the challenges faced by LGBTQ individuals worldwide and to push for change.

Jóhanna played a key role in organizations such as the United Nations and the Council of Europe, where she actively promoted LGBTQ rights as fundamental human rights. Through her advocacy, she helped shape international policies and initiatives aimed at protecting and advancing the rights of LGBTQ individuals. Her contributions paved the way for increased international cooperation and solidarity in the fight for equality.

Inspiring Other LGBTQ Leaders

Jóhanna Sigurðardóttir's rise to power as the world's first openly gay Prime Minister inspired countless LGBTQ individuals to pursue careers in politics and activism. Her success challenged traditional notions of leadership and shattered stereotypes, showing that sexual orientation should never be a barrier to achieving one's goals.

As a trailblazer, Jóhanna became a symbol of hope and resilience for LGBTQ communities worldwide. Her story encouraged others to embrace their true identities and strive for equal rights and representation. By paving the way for future LGBTQ leaders, Jóhanna ensured that her impact would be felt for generations to come.

Transforming Attitudes and Perceptions

Jóhanna's leadership had a profound impact on attitudes and perceptions towards LGBTQ individuals in Iceland and beyond. Through her advocacy and legislative victories, she helped shift societal norms and challenge deeply ingrained prejudices.

By publicly embracing her own identity and living authentically, Jóhanna challenged stereotypes and humanized the LGBTQ experience. Her visibility provided a positive representation for LGBTQ individuals, fostering empathy and understanding within society. As a result, more people embraced the idea of equality and began to question discriminatory beliefs and practices.

Remembering Jóhanna's Contributions

Jóhanna Sigurðardóttir's contributions to LGBTQ rights in Iceland and beyond will forever be remembered. Her dedication to equality, her unwavering commitment to justice, and her resilience in the face of adversity serve as an inspiration to all.

Her legacy is not only in the laws she fought for but also in the hearts and minds she touched. Through her transformative leadership, Jóhanna brought about significant changes in society's perception of LGBTQ individuals. Her advocacy and activism continue to shape LGBTQ rights globally, reminding us that progress is possible when we stand together against injustice and discrimination.

We owe a debt of gratitude to Jóhanna Sigurðardóttir for her extraordinary contributions to the LGBTQ community. Her legacy serves as a beacon of hope, reminding us that our fight for equality is not in vain and that every individual, regardless of sexual orientation or gender identity, deserves to be treated with dignity and respect.

Let us continue to build upon Jóhanna's legacy, honoring her memory by working together to create a world where LGBTQ rights are protected, celebrated, and embraced by all.

Paving the way for future LGBTQ leaders

Jóhanna Sigurðardóttir's political journey not only made her the world's first openly gay Prime Minister but also paved the way for future LGBTQ leaders around the world. By breaking barriers, championing LGBTQ rights, and transforming society, Jóhanna left a lasting impact on the political landscape. Her legacy serves as an inspiration for aspiring politicians and activists, offering valuable lessons for shaping a more inclusive and equitable world.

Empowering LGBTQ Individuals

One of the most significant contributions that Jóhanna made was empowering LGBTQ individuals to embrace their identities and engage in politics. Through her visibility and authenticity, she provided a role model for queer individuals who aspired to be leaders. Her success proved that being true to oneself does not hinder one's ability to excel professionally. Jóhanna's journey taught LGBTQ individuals that they have the power to change the world, regardless of their sexual orientation or gender identity.

Promoting Representation

Representation is essential in creating an inclusive political landscape. Jóhanna's political journey highlighted the importance of LGBTQ representation in positions of power. By occupying the role of Prime Minister, she shattered the glass ceiling and showed that LGBTQ individuals can be successful leaders who bring unique perspectives to the table. This achievement inspired others to run for office, fostering a more diverse and representative political environment.

Advocacy for LGBTQ Rights

Jóhanna's relentless advocacy for LGBTQ rights set a precedent for future LGBTQ leaders. She demonstrated the importance of voicing concerns, fighting for equality, and pushing for legislative changes that protect LGBTQ individuals. Her work in legalizing same-sex marriage, protecting against discrimination, and advocating for adoption rights paved the way for progressive LGBTQ rights globally. Her achievements serve as a roadmap for future LGBTQ leaders to pursue meaningful and impactful policy changes.

Collaboration and Coalition Building

Building alliances and coalitions with like-minded politicians played a crucial role in Jóhanna's success. She showed the significance of forging relationships and working across party lines to advance LGBTQ rights. Future LGBTQ leaders can learn from Jóhanna's ability to form strategic partnerships, navigate political landscapes, and cultivate support to enact meaningful change. Collaboration and coalition building are vital strategies for achieving LGBTQ-friendly policies and fostering societal transformation.

Mobilizing Intersectional Movements

Jóhanna's dedication to LGBTQ rights went beyond advocating for her own community. She understood the importance of intersectional activism, recognizing that progress for one marginalized group benefits society as a whole. Her leadership style embraced a holistic approach, fostering collaboration between LGBTQ communities and other social justice movements. Future LGBTQ leaders can learn from this approach, recognizing the interconnectedness of various social issues and mobilizing diverse groups for collective progress.

Global Influence and Inspiration

Jóhanna's impact extended beyond Iceland. Her historic achievement resonated globally, inspiring LGBTQ individuals to pursue political careers and become catalysts for change in their own countries. Her legacy instills hope and encourages LGBTQ leaders worldwide to use their voices, challenge norms, and fight for equality. The ripple effect of her advocacy reverberates today and will continue to empower future generations of LGBTQ leaders.

In conclusion, through her political journey, Jóhanna Sigurðardóttir paved the way for future LGBTQ leaders by empowering individuals, promoting representation, advocating for LGBTQ rights, building coalitions, mobilizing intersectional movements, and inspiring individuals on a global scale. Her legacy serves as a beacon of hope, encouraging LGBTQ individuals to embrace their identities, pursue political careers, and create a more inclusive society. The world owes a debt of gratitude to Jóhanna for her pioneering spirit and unwavering dedication to equality.

Transforming attitudes and perceptions of LGBTQ individuals

In this section, we delve into the profound impact Jóhanna Sigurðardóttir had on transforming attitudes and perceptions of LGBTQ individuals not only in Iceland but also around the world. Her courage, resilience, and unwavering commitment to equality paved the way for significant social change and challenged longstanding prejudices.

Understanding the societal context

To fully appreciate Jóhanna's transformative impact, we must first understand the societal context in which she operated. In many parts of the world, LGBTQ individuals faced stigmatization, discrimination, and marginalization. Attitudes toward homosexuality were often negative, and there was limited recognition of LGBTQ rights and identities.

Jóhanna recognized the urgent need for change and was determined to challenge the prevailing norms and prejudices. By bringing the LGBTQ community's struggles to the forefront of public discourse, she forced people to confront their biases and reevaluate their perspectives.

Redefining stereotypes and breaking down barriers

Jóhanna's leadership and visibility shattered stereotypes surrounding LGBTQ individuals. As the first openly gay Prime Minister in the world, she challenged prevailing notions that LGBTQ people could not hold positions of power or responsibility. Through her actions, Jóhanna proved that sexual orientation does not define a person's ability to lead effectively.

Her journey also highlighted the strength, resilience, and contributions of LGBTQ individuals throughout society. By demonstrating her competence and dedication to her role, Jóhanna shattered preconceived notions and proved that LGBTQ individuals are as capable and worthy as anyone else.

Promoting understanding and empathy

A significant aspect of Jóhanna's legacy lies in her ability to foster understanding and empathy among the general population. Through her advocacy, she helped people see that LGBTQ individuals are not a faceless "other" but rather their friends, family members, and neighbors. She humanized the LGBTQ experience, encouraging people to embrace diversity and stand against discrimination.

Jóhanna's commitment to education and awareness was crucial for transforming attitudes. She recognized that people's fear and prejudice often stem from ignorance and lack of exposure. She championed LGBTQ-inclusive education, aimed at dispelling stereotypes and fostering acceptance from an early age.

Celebrating diversity and promoting inclusion

One of the most powerful ways Jóhanna transformed attitudes was by championing a culture of celebration and inclusion. She fought for the recognition and celebration of LGBTQ identities, challenging the notion that being queer was something to be ashamed of.

Through public events, festivals, and pride parades, Jóhanna created spaces where LGBTQ individuals could express themselves openly and unapologetically.

These celebrations not only bolstered a sense of community and belonging but also allowed society at large to witness and celebrate LGBTQ individuals' contributions to the cultural fabric.

Collaboration and dialogue

Jóhanna understood the importance of collaboration and dialogue in transforming attitudes toward LGBTQ individuals. She actively engaged with different stakeholders, including religious leaders, politicians, and community organizations, to bridge divides and foster a deeper understanding of LGBTQ issues.

By creating spaces for open discussions and challenging misconceptions, Jóhanna encouraged productive dialogue that led to empathy and greater acceptance. Her ability to engage people from diverse backgrounds and listen to their concerns allowed her to build bridges and find common ground.

Long-lasting impact

Jóhanna's advocacy and leadership continue to resonate far beyond her time as Prime Minister. Iceland's groundbreaking legislative changes, including legalizing same-sex marriage and protecting LGBTQ individuals from discrimination, have served as inspiration for other nations.

Her legacy also lives on in the countless LGBTQ individuals who have found the strength to embrace their identities and fight for equality. Jóhanna's story empowers others to challenge societal norms and work towards creating a more inclusive and accepting world.

In conclusion, Jóhanna Sigurðardóttir's transformative impact on attitudes and perceptions of LGBTQ individuals is immeasurable. Through her courage, resilience, and unwavering commitment, she shattered stereotypes, fostered understanding, and celebrated diversity. Her legacy serves as a testament to the power of one person's determination to effect change and inspires generations to come.

Remembering Jóhanna's contributions to society

Jóhanna Sigurðardóttir's tenure as the first openly gay Prime Minister of Iceland left an indelible mark on society. Her commitment to LGBTQ rights, along with her leadership during political upheavals and challenging economic times, solidified her legacy as a transformative figure.

Jóhanna's impact on society can be seen in multiple areas, from legislative victories to changing attitudes and perceptions of LGBTQ individuals. Let's explore her contributions in more detail:

Shaping LGBTQ rights in Iceland and beyond

Jóhanna's most significant contribution lies in the advancements she made for LGBTQ rights in Iceland. As Prime Minister, she played a pivotal role in legalizing same-sex marriage in 2010, making Iceland one of the first countries to grant full marriage equality. This landmark legislation not only provided LGBTQ couples with the legal recognition they deserved but also set a powerful example for other nations to follow.

Moreover, Jóhanna worked tirelessly to protect LGBTQ individuals from discrimination. Her government implemented robust anti-discrimination laws, ensuring that LGBTQ individuals enjoyed the same rights and opportunities as their heterosexual counterparts. These measures contributed to a more inclusive and equitable society, where individuals can live authentically without fear of prejudice.

Jóhanna's accomplishments did not stop at Iceland's borders. Her progressive policies and advocacy efforts inspired LGBTQ activists worldwide, serving as a beacon of hope and a model for change. Many countries took cues from Iceland's success and introduced similar legislation, affirming LGBTQ rights, and fostering greater acceptance in their own societies.

Paving the way for future LGBTQ leaders

Jóhanna's rise to power shattered traditional stereotypes and proved that sexual orientation should never be a barrier to leadership. Her journey from community activism to becoming the head of government inspired countless LGBTQ individuals to pursue careers in politics and public service.

By openly embracing her identity, Jóhanna showed that LGBTQ leaders can bring unique perspectives and experiences to the table, making them valuable assets in the decision-making processes. Her courage and determination demonstrated that one's sexual orientation should never limit their potential to effect change and contribute to society.

Jóhanna's political success also served as a reminder for LGBTQ individuals that they are not alone. She became a symbol of hope, demonstrating that it is possible to overcome adversity and achieve greatness, even in the face of societal prejudices.

Her leadership inspired a new generation of LGBTQ activists and politicians, eager to follow in her footsteps and continue fighting for equality and justice.

Transforming attitudes and perceptions of LGBTQ individuals

One of Jóhanna's key achievements was her ability to challenge societal attitudes and perceptions towards LGBTQ individuals. Through her visibility as a political leader, she helped humanize the LGBTQ community and dispel harmful stereotypes.

Her dedication to equality and inclusivity resonated with the public, gradually eroding homophobia and fostering greater acceptance. Jóhanna's authentic and compassionate leadership style debunked misconceptions, encouraging people to see LGBTQ individuals as equals deserving of respect and equal rights.

Moreover, Jóhanna's policies actively promoted dialogue and understanding between different segments of society. By encouraging openness and empathy, she fostered a more cohesive and tolerant nation, where diversity is celebrated and embraced.

The legacy of inclusive policies

Jóhanna's legacy extends far beyond her time in office. Her inclusive policies and legislative victories continue to shape Iceland's social and political landscape, ensuring a more equitable society for generations to come.

The legal recognition of same-sex marriage, comprehensive anti-discrimination laws, and LGBTQ-inclusive adoption policies are enduring testaments to Jóhanna's commitment to equality. These legislative changes have created a more just society, where LGBTQ individuals have the freedom to love, work, and raise families without fear of discrimination or prejudice.

Jóhanna's legacy also serves as a reminder of the power of activism and advocacy. Her journey from an activist within the LGBTQ community to the highest office in the land illustrates the immense impact individuals can have in driving social change. It encourages future activists to fight for equality and challenges lawmakers to enact laws that protect and honor the rights of all citizens.

In conclusion, Jóhanna Sigurðardóttir's contributions to society as Iceland's first openly gay Prime Minister are immeasurable. Through her determination, leadership, and progressive policies, she shaped the landscape of LGBTQ rights in Iceland and beyond, paved the way for future LGBTQ leaders, transformed attitudes and perceptions, and left a lasting legacy of inclusivity. Her story continues to inspire and empower individuals around the world to fight for equality and justice, reminding us that change is possible when we dare to challenge the status quo.

Index

-doubt, 5

a, 1–7, 9–29, 31–53, 55–74, 77, 80–85, 87–95, 97–108, 111–121
ability, 7, 12, 16, 20, 21, 26, 32, 33, 40–42, 44, 46, 47, 50, 51, 53, 57, 58, 61, 62, 65–68, 70, 73, 93, 98–100, 102, 105–108, 116, 118, 119, 121
academia, 71
acceptance, 1–7, 9, 11–16, 19, 22, 27–29, 34, 50, 59, 60, 63, 73, 80–83, 87–91, 93, 94, 111, 112, 114, 118–121
access, 27, 44, 67, 72, 83, 94, 98, 107
accessibility, 40, 67, 103
accountability, 43, 45, 56, 64, 107
achievement, 46, 62, 81, 93, 101, 112, 116, 117
act, 69, 83, 103, 105
action, 16, 17, 29, 36, 42, 48, 56, 66, 67, 107
activism, 2, 4, 6, 7, 11–15, 18, 20, 21, 23, 26, 27, 31, 33–35, 47, 51–53, 63, 84, 85, 87–89, 112–115, 117, 120, 121
activist, 13, 16, 21, 23, 25, 27, 31, 49, 51–53, 64, 82, 100, 101, 121
activity, 91
actor, 72
acumen, 55, 65
addition, 17, 46, 88, 94
admiration, 40, 42, 57
adoption, 21, 26, 60, 85–87, 116, 121
advancement, 28, 83, 95, 112
advantage, 109
adversity, 2, 3, 5, 7, 10, 11, 13–16, 21, 24, 26, 41, 42, 45, 57, 61, 84, 98–100, 115, 120
advice, 105
advocacy, 2, 4, 9, 14–17, 20, 21, 23–27, 29, 33, 35, 46–48, 68, 73, 77, 82–84, 87, 89, 95, 111, 113–121
advocate, 3, 5, 7, 10, 13, 15–18, 20–23, 25, 26, 28, 31–36, 39, 44, 53, 58, 62, 82, 92, 94, 95, 99, 114
affection, 18
affiliation, 51, 69
aftermath, 56, 57, 59, 61, 62, 65

age, 1, 17, 28, 64, 94, 118
agenda, 9, 36, 42, 46, 58, 64, 94,
    105, 109
alienation, 10
alternative, 58
anchor, 99
appearance, 108
appointment, 23, 61
approach, 17, 18, 24, 29, 37, 40, 42,
    44, 45, 48, 50, 51, 53, 59,
    61, 66–68, 70, 74, 81, 84,
    90, 91, 93–95, 98, 102,
    106, 107, 117
arena, 33, 39, 40, 46, 52, 73
argument, 38
art, 15, 18
ascent, 55, 62, 112
aspect, 22, 43, 45, 49, 93, 100,
    103–105, 118
asset, 59
assistance, 27, 28, 70
atmosphere, 11
attention, 18, 39, 45, 47, 74, 99, 100,
    104, 105, 108, 109
audience, 13, 17, 18, 24, 26, 106
austerity, 56, 70
authenticity, 9, 14, 45, 63, 103, 113,
    116
authority, 105
awareness, 11, 13, 15, 18, 20, 22, 24,
    25, 28, 29, 47, 50, 52, 60,
    74, 81, 83, 88, 89, 92, 114,
    118

backdrop, 55
background, 56, 80
backlash, 2, 6, 108
balance, 20, 21, 33, 35, 47, 51–53,
    97, 98, 101–103, 108

balancing, 20, 21, 33, 35, 47, 99,
    101–103, 105
banking, 56, 65–68, 70
barrier, 46, 112, 114, 120
base, 105
basis, 2
battle, 81, 83
beacon, 13, 16, 20, 32, 45, 74, 84,
    93, 112, 115, 117, 120
bearing, 12
behavior, 84
being, 3, 4, 6, 13–15, 19, 25, 34–36,
    43, 45, 52, 62–64, 67, 68,
    87, 88, 98, 99, 101–105,
    108, 116, 118
belief, 7, 10, 39, 58, 59
belonging, 17, 49, 82, 91, 93, 119
bigotry, 41
bill, 35
birth, 55
bitterness, 15
bond, 97, 100
box, 42
boy, 90
branch, 57
breaking, 6, 7, 12, 16, 22, 29, 47, 51,
    62, 83, 112, 115
bridge, 21, 37, 40, 44, 49, 53, 56, 62,
    90, 91, 119
budget, 70
building, 17, 18, 23, 25, 27, 35, 37,
    40, 42, 44–46, 49–51, 56,
    58, 59, 63, 65, 67, 69, 91,
    106, 116, 117
burden, 27, 70
business, 72

campaign, 44
candidate, 66

capital, 67
care, 52, 98, 99, 102–105
career, 3, 12, 19, 28, 33, 34, 42, 59, 61, 66, 68, 98, 99, 106
case, 6, 21, 23, 67
cast, 90
catalyst, 3, 82, 83
cause, 4, 16, 22–25, 32, 38, 44, 63, 64, 94
ceiling, 112, 116
celebration, 93, 118
century, 7
chain, 18
challenge, 4, 6, 8, 10, 12–14, 17, 18, 20, 21, 28, 33–35, 45, 47, 51, 52, 55, 60, 62, 64, 85, 88–90, 92, 100, 101, 106–108, 112, 113, 115, 117–119, 121, 122
champion, 9, 19, 33, 38, 45, 46, 58, 80, 94, 108
championing, 22, 44, 47, 48, 51, 84, 87, 113, 115, 118
change, 2–4, 7–10, 13–26, 28, 29, 31–36, 38, 39, 45–53, 55, 58, 60, 61, 65, 66, 73, 74, 77, 80, 82–85, 87, 89, 90, 92–94, 99, 100, 106, 109, 111, 113, 114, 116–122
channel, 14, 43
chapter, 3, 9, 31, 33, 39, 55, 57, 77, 80, 97, 105, 111
characteristic, 56
child, 85
circle, 101, 104
citizen, 59
clarity, 98
class, 59
climate, 36

coalition, 17, 22, 47, 58, 59, 62–65, 67, 69, 116
collaboration, 20, 21, 24–26, 33–35, 37, 46, 48–51, 58, 69, 71–73, 92, 93, 95, 117, 119
collapse, 57, 58, 67
combat, 11, 83
combination, 105
commitment, 9, 20, 21, 23, 24, 27, 32, 37, 39, 40, 42, 43, 47, 52, 53, 55, 57–63, 65–70, 72, 74, 81–83, 87, 93–95, 106, 107, 112–115, 117–119, 121
communication, 16–18, 32, 43, 67, 100, 106, 107
community, 3, 4, 9–11, 13, 15–20, 22–29, 31, 34, 38, 39, 41, 43, 45–48, 51–53, 58–60, 62, 64, 70, 80–84, 89, 91–95, 105, 111–115, 117–121
companionship, 99, 104
compassion, 6, 52, 89, 103, 112
competence, 40, 46, 56, 66, 112, 118
competitiveness, 71
component, 16, 51, 89
composure, 105
compromise, 21, 35, 47, 58, 102
concept, 18
conclusion, 7, 20, 27, 29, 42, 47, 48, 60, 88, 93, 100, 107, 109, 113, 117, 119, 121
conference, 24
confidence, 6, 21, 24, 32, 62, 66, 68, 70
conflict, 4, 108, 109
confusion, 1, 5, 10

connection, 16, 40, 103
consensus, 40, 64, 69, 91
consequence, 67
conservation, 72
constituency, 40, 44
content, 28
context, 57, 83, 91, 117
contribution, 94, 120
control, 66, 101, 108, 109
controversy, 101, 108
conviction, 98, 113
cooperation, 70, 72, 114
core, 59
corruption, 106, 107
counseling, 28
counter, 105, 106
country, 27, 29, 33, 35, 38, 55–63, 65, 66, 68–74, 80, 81, 88, 93, 94, 106, 111, 113, 114
couple, 100
courage, 4–7, 21, 41, 45, 47, 113, 117, 119, 120
course, 41, 48, 59
coverage, 108, 109
creation, 29, 67, 71, 72
credibility, 26, 105, 108
credit, 67
crime, 28, 34
crisis, 55–59, 61–63, 65–73
criticism, 41, 42, 48, 57, 60, 70, 98, 100, 105–108
crunch, 67
culture, 71, 83, 108, 118
curriculum, 94

dance, 97
debt, 65, 68, 115, 117
debunk, 28, 92

decision, 32, 35, 39, 43, 51, 65, 68, 95, 101, 107, 111, 120
decline, 66
dedication, 4, 22, 26, 32, 39–41, 43, 46–48, 60, 63, 66, 84, 98, 100, 111, 115, 117, 118, 121
deficit, 70
demand, 73
depth, 108
desire, 2, 31, 34
despair, 15
destination, 71
detail, 120
determination, 1, 3, 6, 12–15, 20, 32, 33, 36, 39–43, 45, 55, 56, 59–61, 63, 65, 68, 69, 73, 82, 95, 105, 107, 119–121
deterrent, 83, 84
development, 28, 37, 44, 69, 71–73
dialogue, 11, 18, 20, 22, 28, 37, 40, 47–50, 56, 60, 64, 67, 69, 88–90, 92, 93, 95, 106, 112, 119, 121
difference, 11, 14, 27, 29, 33, 36, 39, 63, 104
dignity, 22, 82, 113, 115
dilemma, 101
diplomacy, 35, 49
disarray, 55
discontent, 58, 59
discourse, 29, 33, 74, 108, 118
discovery, 1, 3, 5, 10, 12, 14, 90
discrimination, 1–7, 10–13, 15, 18, 19, 21, 25, 26, 28, 29, 34, 39, 41, 45, 46, 48, 59–61, 63, 66, 74, 82–84, 88, 89,

Index

91, 93, 94, 97, 105, 106, 108, 111, 114–121
distortion, 108
diversification, 68, 112
diversity, 13, 29, 74, 83, 93, 118, 119, 121
doubt, 5
drive, 7, 14, 44, 73
duty, 47
dynamic, 37

economic, 35, 36, 44, 49, 57–59, 61–63, 65–69, 71–73, 119
economy, 55–58, 61, 62, 65–72
ecosystem, 72
education, 12, 28, 29, 44, 52, 60, 71, 83, 84, 89, 90, 92–94, 111, 118
effect, 13, 15, 31, 33, 46–49, 51, 52, 82, 117, 119, 120
effort, 25, 40, 46, 73, 83, 90, 100
element, 59
empathy, 11, 15–17, 23–25, 29, 40, 43, 50, 51, 56, 60, 61, 63, 64, 83, 89–92, 112, 115, 118, 119, 121
emphasis, 58, 72, 74
employment, 48, 59, 67, 83, 94, 111, 114
empowerment, 2
encouragement, 9–11, 24
endeavor, 48, 81, 102
energy, 4, 14, 37, 53, 66, 68, 71–73, 98
enforcement, 83, 84
engagement, 17, 22, 36, 37, 40, 82, 112
entrepreneurship, 71

environment, 10–12, 28, 56, 57, 69, 71, 87, 88, 108, 112, 116
equality, 2, 3, 6, 8, 9, 13, 15, 18–29, 31–35, 39, 41, 46, 47, 49, 50, 52, 55, 59, 60, 64, 68, 73, 74, 80–84, 87, 88, 91–95, 105, 106, 111, 113–117, 119–122
era, 55
error, 98
establishment, 28, 61
esteem, 6
ethic, 41, 61
event, 24, 38
evidence, 23, 37, 48
example, 14, 16, 18, 20, 24, 47, 53, 80, 82, 87, 88, 91, 100, 109, 120
exception, 23, 63, 100, 105
exchange, 72, 73, 89
excitement, 101
exclusion, 85, 88
exercise, 91, 102
existence, 33
experience, 12, 16, 29, 38, 66, 90, 91, 93, 115, 118
expert, 37
expertise, 58, 61
exposure, 89, 90, 118
extent, 65
eye, 97–100, 102–105

fabric, 119
face, 2, 6, 11, 13, 15–17, 21, 24, 27, 36, 40–42, 49, 84, 91, 97, 98, 100, 101, 115, 120
fairness, 49, 82
faith, 66, 68
fallout, 107

family, 2, 4, 6, 7, 9–14, 23, 24, 60, 81, 83, 84, 87, 90, 97, 101, 104, 107, 118
favor, 88
fear, 1, 5, 7, 10, 32, 46, 60, 84, 88, 94, 118, 120, 121
feat, 45
fellow, 15, 20, 23, 48, 49, 66
field, 29
fight, 3, 4, 6, 7, 13, 15, 16, 19–23, 27, 29, 39, 41, 46, 73, 74, 80, 82, 83, 87, 105, 114, 115, 117, 119, 121
fighting, 5, 13, 18, 20, 23, 42, 60, 113, 116, 121
figure, 27, 29, 39, 41, 53, 58, 61, 62, 66, 74, 80, 98, 100, 101, 103, 105, 106, 119
figurehead, 73
fil, 18
film, 90
finding, 17, 37, 39, 44, 47, 50, 53, 64, 91, 98, 100, 101, 103
flash, 18
focus, 41, 68, 82, 84, 98, 99, 102, 108
food, 18
force, 2, 4, 13, 15, 17, 38, 39, 47, 82
forefront, 9, 63, 93, 95, 109, 112, 118
form, 16, 22, 24, 34, 69, 116
formation, 73
foster, 22, 28, 29, 43, 50, 52, 71, 81, 89, 92, 93, 106, 118, 119
foundation, 11, 12, 14, 36, 43, 59, 64, 66, 67, 69, 70, 72, 80, 100
framework, 36
freedom, 10, 22, 81, 121

front, 22, 56, 69, 73
fuel, 3, 4, 6, 10, 13–15, 26, 42
fulfillment, 14, 98–100, 102
funding, 71, 72, 95
future, 6, 11, 12, 20, 22, 26, 27, 29, 32, 33, 45, 46, 50, 51, 53, 56, 58, 60, 61, 63, 66, 68–71, 80, 84, 88, 90, 93–95, 103, 107, 111, 113–117, 121

gain, 23–26, 32, 36, 37, 40, 41, 43, 45, 49, 58, 65, 67, 69, 89, 91, 102, 106
gap, 21, 27, 53, 90
Geir H. Haarde, 58
gender, 6–8, 10, 12, 14, 19, 24, 27, 28, 33, 48, 59, 83, 88, 89, 94, 114–116
generation, 9, 15, 27, 112, 121
gesture, 47
girl, 10
glass, 112, 116
glimpse, 90
goal, 36, 49, 50, 61
governance, 47, 67, 68
government, 55–59, 66–72, 95, 111, 120
grace, 21, 41, 92, 99, 100, 102, 105
gratitude, 115, 117
greatness, 120
ground, 20, 37, 44, 50, 61, 81, 91–93, 119
groundbreaking, 21, 32, 40, 48, 80, 83, 93, 101, 119
groundwork, 11, 71, 106
group, 90, 117
growth, 1, 7, 12, 14, 19, 42, 62, 66, 69–72, 98, 99

Index

guidance, 11, 17, 23, 24, 101, 105, 107
hall, 17, 43, 65, 67, 69, 92
hand, 19
handling, 68
happiness, 1, 4, 6, 14, 19, 98–103
harassment, 83
harmony, 102
hate, 28, 34
haven, 2
head, 2, 4, 7, 15, 16, 48, 57, 99, 105, 107, 120
headline, 108
health, 91, 104, 109
healthcare, 44, 111
heteronormativity, 14
hiking, 104
history, 38, 62, 84, 94, 111
hit, 57, 66, 68, 90
holding, 51, 53, 112
home, 11, 39
homophobia, 1, 5, 6, 14, 121
homosexuality, 1, 2, 118
hope, 13, 16, 20, 21, 29, 32, 45, 57, 73, 74, 84, 112, 114, 115, 117, 120
hostility, 51
housing, 48, 59, 83, 94, 111, 114
hurdle, 41

Iceland, 1, 2, 7, 9, 10, 19, 20, 22, 23, 27–29, 32, 36, 42, 45–48, 53, 55–63, 65–74, 77, 80–84, 87–89, 91, 93–95, 105, 106, 111–115, 117, 119–121
Iceland, 80
idea, 2, 46, 115
identity, 1–7, 9, 10, 12, 14, 19, 28, 32–34, 41, 45, 59, 83, 88, 89, 91, 94, 105, 114–116, 120
ideology, 39
ignorance, 118
image, 108
impact, 9, 12, 13, 16, 18, 19, 22, 25–29, 34, 36–38, 41, 47, 49, 52, 53, 57, 60, 65, 67, 68, 73, 74, 77, 80, 82–84, 87, 88, 95, 102, 105, 106, 111–115, 117, 119–121
implementation, 59, 83, 87–89
importance, 3, 5, 11, 12, 16, 20–22, 24, 25, 27–29, 33–36, 43, 46–50, 52, 56, 58, 60, 63, 64, 66, 67, 69, 71, 74, 81, 82, 92, 93, 95, 97, 98, 100, 103, 106, 108, 116, 117, 119
inclusion, 49, 62, 87, 91, 93, 118
inclusivity, 13, 18, 22, 25, 27, 29, 34, 48, 53, 57, 59, 64, 69, 73, 74, 87, 88, 93, 94, 108, 112, 121
income, 27
increase, 67, 112
indifference, 51
individual, 7, 9, 12, 19, 24, 32, 36, 43, 49, 51, 91, 101, 115
industry, 71
inequality, 27, 35, 61
inflation, 70
influence, 15, 18, 20, 21, 25–27, 29, 34–38, 41, 45, 46, 48, 52, 64, 66, 73, 81, 85, 90, 111, 112, 114
information, 28, 39, 92, 108

infrastructure, 66, 71
initiative, 94
injustice, 115
innovation, 57, 66, 68, 71, 73
input, 24, 52, 69
insecurity, 5
inspiration, 5, 7, 10, 13, 29, 32, 33, 41, 42, 47, 50, 60, 63, 65, 74, 82, 88, 93, 95, 97, 102, 113, 115, 119
instability, 66
instance, 90
institution, 81, 87
integration, 94
integrity, 43, 44, 106, 107
intelligence, 46, 61
interconnectedness, 117
intersectionality, 18, 35
introspection, 12
intrusion, 99, 103, 104
intrusiveness, 100
invasion, 100
investigation, 107
investment, 70–72
investor, 62
involvement, 29, 61, 107
island, 93
isolation, 1, 10
issue, 27, 49, 59, 80, 82, 107, 112

Jennifer Smith, 38
job, 67, 68, 71, 72
journey, 1–16, 20, 21, 23–26, 29, 31–34, 36, 39–43, 45, 47, 49, 51, 55, 56, 59–63, 65, 66, 80, 82, 90, 95, 97, 99, 100, 102, 103, 105, 112, 113, 115–118, 120, 121
joy, 83, 93, 98, 99

judgment, 2, 6, 7, 10, 11, 97, 108
justice, 2, 6, 15, 17, 21, 24, 27, 28, 31, 33, 36, 39, 49, 55, 58, 59, 61, 62, 84, 92, 105, 113, 115, 117, 121, 122
Jóhanna, 1–16, 18–29, 31–36, 39–53, 55–74, 81–85, 91–93, 97–109, 111–121
Jóhanna Sigurðardóttir, 1, 5, 7–9, 13, 14, 19, 20, 22, 25, 27, 29, 31, 33, 34, 36, 39, 41, 43, 45, 47, 49, 51, 55, 57–61, 63, 65–68, 70, 74, 77, 80–84, 87, 89, 91, 93, 94, 97, 99, 101, 103–106, 108, 109, 111, 115, 117
Jóhanna Sigurðardóttir's, 1, 5, 7, 9, 11, 16, 18, 20, 22, 23, 27, 31–33, 39, 40, 42, 45, 47–49, 51, 53, 57, 59, 60, 62, 65–68, 72, 73, 80, 82–84, 89, 95, 99, 100, 102, 107, 111–115, 119, 121
Jóhanna Sigurðardóttir, 3
Jónína, 99, 100
Jónína Leósdóttir, 97, 99, 100

key, 5, 17, 19, 22, 23, 27, 32, 34, 37, 38, 41, 43, 47, 51, 59, 66, 85, 86, 89, 93, 99, 101, 114, 121
kiss, 18
knowledge, 41, 63, 71, 89, 92

lack, 92, 118
ladder, 40
land, 121

landmark, 46, 81, 83, 84, 93, 111, 120
landscape, 21, 23, 26, 32, 34, 36, 41, 47, 53, 55–57, 59, 61, 63, 65, 68, 80, 81, 105, 108, 112, 115, 116, 121
law, 28, 35, 81, 111
leader, 25, 29, 32, 33, 40, 42–44, 48, 58, 63, 64, 66, 68, 72, 73, 82, 88, 99, 101, 111, 121
leadership, 11, 28, 29, 32, 35, 37, 39, 40, 43, 45, 46, 55–59, 61–63, 66–70, 72–74, 81, 83, 93–95, 99, 107, 111–115, 117–121
learning, 40, 42, 91, 95, 99, 102, 107
legacy, 9, 20, 22, 27, 29, 48, 53, 60, 63, 68, 73, 74, 80, 82, 84, 87, 93, 100, 103, 106, 111–113, 115, 117–119, 121
legalization, 19, 21, 22, 59, 60, 80–82, 87–89, 113
legislation, 13, 15, 20–22, 26–29, 34–36, 47, 48, 50, 60, 73, 81, 83, 84, 92, 93, 95, 114, 120
legitimacy, 64
level, 17, 24, 31, 39, 51, 65, 91, 100, 102, 112
life, 4, 6, 9, 12, 13, 16, 19, 26, 43, 48, 59, 83, 89–95, 97–101, 103, 104, 107–109, 111
lifeblood, 36
limit, 108, 120
line, 33, 101, 108
Lisa Thompson, 38
lobby, 50
lobbying, 18, 50, 81

love, 4, 6, 9–12, 14, 22, 23, 46, 59, 63, 82, 83, 87, 90, 93, 97, 99, 100, 121
loyalty, 40

magnitude, 65, 67
making, 14, 23, 27, 35, 36, 39, 43, 48, 51, 65, 68–70, 81, 85, 93, 95, 98, 102, 106, 107, 111, 120
man, 7, 14, 48
management, 67
managing, 56, 65, 67, 97, 99, 105
marginalization, 89, 117
mark, 20, 22, 27, 47, 63, 84, 113, 119
marriage, 7, 19, 21–23, 26, 46–48, 59, 60, 73, 80–84, 87–89, 93, 94, 106, 111, 113, 114, 116, 119–121
mask, 14
master, 105
matter, 11, 22, 37, 49, 59, 112
means, 25
media, 18, 22, 25, 26, 29, 38, 39, 48, 50, 52, 64, 65, 89, 90, 98–100, 103–109
meditation, 102
meeting, 38, 98, 101
member, 11, 19, 58, 90
memory, 115
mentorship, 27, 72
message, 17, 28, 38, 46, 50, 59, 64, 73, 87–89, 93, 94, 109
midst, 65, 73
milestone, 55, 61, 80, 81
mind, 55, 85, 93
mindedness, 89
mindfulness, 99

mindset, 53, 102
minister, 31, 82, 94, 108
mission, 40
mobilization, 16–18
model, 21, 74, 114, 116, 120
moment, 16, 55, 62, 81
momentum, 29, 33, 50
motivation, 3–5, 7, 10, 13–16, 26, 41, 42, 45
motivator, 98
move, 90, 99
movement, 4, 15, 16, 18, 23, 24, 27, 36, 38, 82, 92, 93
movie, 90

narrative, 16, 49, 51, 64, 106, 108, 109
nation, 2, 55–57, 62, 65, 69, 93, 106, 121
nature, 45, 98
navigation, 32
necessity, 70
need, 19, 25, 35, 48, 50, 55, 58, 71, 73, 84, 91, 95, 104, 118
negativity, 13, 42, 108
negotiation, 48, 50
network, 21, 23, 25, 27, 29, 35, 41, 42, 46, 49, 51, 105–107
newfound, 42
news, 73
norm, 14
notice, 38, 73
notion, 118

objective, 53
obsession, 108
obstacle, 100

office, 31, 32, 41, 56, 59, 63, 65, 69, 74, 97, 99, 105, 106, 112, 113, 116, 121
on, 1, 2, 4–7, 9, 10, 12, 14–20, 22–24, 26–29, 32–42, 44–53, 55, 57–63, 65–74, 82–84, 87, 88, 90, 91, 94, 95, 97, 99–102, 104–109, 111–115, 117, 119, 120
one, 1, 4, 8, 9, 12, 14, 19, 31, 32, 36, 46, 47, 49, 53, 55, 59, 60, 68, 80, 83, 89, 94, 108, 114, 116, 117, 119, 120
opening, 72
openness, 103, 121
opinion, 26, 29, 35, 50, 64, 81, 90, 108
opportunity, 18, 26, 27, 34, 36, 42, 87
opposition, 15, 22, 23, 40–42, 48–50, 60, 81, 82, 98, 100, 105, 106
oppression, 18
order, 25, 48, 57, 58, 62, 69, 70, 91
organization, 16
organizing, 16–18, 20, 38
orientation, 1, 2, 5, 6, 11, 13, 19, 27, 28, 32, 33, 40, 41, 46, 47, 56, 59, 83, 88, 89, 94, 105, 112, 114–116, 118, 120
other, 17, 18, 20, 22–24, 29, 48–51, 56, 60, 67, 69, 72–74, 80, 82, 84, 88, 90–95, 100, 102, 111, 114, 117–120
output, 66
outreach, 18
outset, 58
over, 56, 67, 71, 108
overview, 57

Index

ownership, 67

parent, 85
parenting, 87
part, 17, 34, 36, 42, 105
participant, 4
participation, 72, 90
partner, 97, 99
partnership, 83, 100
party, 36–40, 49, 51, 56, 62, 67, 106, 107, 116
passage, 26, 48, 50, 83
passion, 2–4, 25, 31, 39, 53, 61, 100
path, 3, 4, 6, 9, 14, 36, 40, 42, 51, 55, 60, 62, 65, 70, 72, 102
patience, 90
pay, 27
peace, 102
people, 3, 26, 28, 29, 40, 43, 44, 46, 56, 58, 62, 63, 65, 67–69, 89, 91–93, 98, 106, 112, 115, 118, 119, 121
perception, 52, 109, 115
perfection, 102
period, 5, 57, 111
perseverance, 13, 31, 49, 60, 61, 63, 113
person, 1, 53, 83, 118, 119
persona, 108
perspective, 7, 53, 60, 102
piece, 94
pillar, 100
place, 1, 11, 93, 104
plan, 66
planning, 17, 48
platform, 13, 15, 17, 20, 23, 25–27, 31, 34, 36, 39, 47, 52, 57, 92, 105
play, 17, 36, 89, 108, 109

point, 98
policy, 18, 23, 27, 36–42, 52, 84, 94, 103, 108, 109, 116
policymaking, 95
politician, 13, 15, 20, 21, 23, 31, 32, 34, 35, 41–49, 51, 59, 61, 66, 67, 97, 100
pool, 49
population, 44, 61, 64, 118
position, 19, 20, 25, 28, 33, 35, 40, 43, 44, 46, 48, 51, 56, 62, 64, 68, 72, 94, 112, 114
potential, 6, 12, 31, 33–37, 39, 41, 52, 63, 66, 71, 101, 108, 113, 120
poverty, 35, 67
power, 1, 11, 12, 16, 18, 23–26, 31, 33–36, 39, 40, 42, 45, 46, 48, 50, 51, 57, 58, 61, 63, 65, 74, 88, 90, 92, 105, 106, 108, 109, 112–114, 116, 118–121
practice, 11
praise, 105
precedent, 48, 82, 111, 116
prejudice, 2, 4, 6, 10–13, 15, 26, 41, 45, 46, 60, 61, 66, 74, 84, 88, 91, 105, 118, 120, 121
presence, 32, 46
pressure, 2, 5–7, 14, 38, 50, 68, 101, 106, 108
pride, 93, 118
principle, 23, 81
priority, 26, 43, 97
privacy, 98, 99, 103–105, 107, 108
problem, 42
process, 5, 7, 12, 31, 32, 39, 43, 62, 65–67, 69, 81, 85, 90, 107, 112

profession, 103
progress, 9, 29, 32, 34, 35, 53, 59–62, 68, 73, 74, 80, 82, 84, 91, 93, 95, 106, 108, 112, 115, 117
prominence, 25
prosperity, 57, 62
protagonist, 90
protection, 10, 21, 24, 28, 34, 35, 47, 60, 70, 72, 83
protest, 18
public, 9, 13, 15, 18, 22–26, 29, 35, 40, 41, 43, 46, 48, 50, 52, 56, 58–60, 62, 64–67, 69, 70, 74, 81–83, 89, 90, 92, 93, 95, 97–109, 112, 114, 118, 120, 121
pursuit, 27, 31, 35, 50, 55, 59, 82, 84, 108
push, 19, 24, 35, 44, 49, 80, 94, 95, 111, 114
puzzle, 94

quality, 19, 52, 98, 104
quest, 2
question, 4, 5, 105, 115
questioning, 1, 107
quo, 15, 18, 42, 46, 113, 122

radio, 92
rally, 58, 64
range, 18, 20, 37, 58, 67, 91
rapport, 37
reach, 18, 23, 26, 65, 106
reading, 104
reality, 48, 60
realization, 2, 14, 31, 33, 35, 39, 40, 84
realm, 112

rebuilding, 62, 70, 72
recession, 66
recognition, 19, 21, 23, 25–27, 34, 47, 48, 60–62, 66, 67, 70, 73, 80, 82, 83, 87–89, 114, 118, 120, 121
record, 58
recovery, 56, 57, 59, 62, 67–71
reestablishment, 72
reflection, 1, 5, 6, 14, 42, 98, 102
reform, 44, 61
refusal, 9
region, 38
relation, 111
relationship, 85, 91, 97, 100
relaxation, 52
reliance, 71
relief, 83
reminder, 47, 48, 84, 112, 120, 121
reporting, 108
representation, 28, 29, 32–34, 47, 57, 89, 90, 112–117
representative, 32, 116
reputation, 26, 59, 62, 66, 68, 72, 106, 108
research, 23, 48, 71, 72
resignation, 58
resilience, 1, 3, 6, 9, 10, 12–17, 21, 31, 32, 39, 41, 42, 45, 47, 55, 60, 63, 67, 68, 70, 72, 73, 99, 100, 102, 103, 106–108, 113–115, 117–119
resistance, 26, 32, 40, 41, 56, 57, 69, 70, 84, 105
resolve, 15, 56, 57, 98
respect, 28, 32, 40, 42, 43, 48, 57, 61, 62, 66, 67, 70, 73, 89,

90, 92, 94, 100, 114, 115, 121
respite, 99
response, 13
responsibility, 39, 72, 98, 118
rest, 59, 88
restaurant, 18
restructuring, 66
result, 25, 112, 115
resurgence, 71, 72
revenue, 71
rhetoric, 46
right, 16, 39, 47, 83, 103, 111
rise, 10, 15, 33, 39, 57, 58, 61, 67, 89, 105, 106, 114, 120
risk, 103
road, 63
roadmap, 50, 80, 116
Robert Johnson, 38
role, 2, 6, 9, 11, 13, 14, 17, 19–23, 29, 33, 36, 38–40, 44, 47, 48, 51, 56, 58, 59, 62, 68, 70, 77, 82, 85, 87, 89–91, 93–95, 98, 99, 101, 104, 107, 108, 111, 113, 114, 116, 118, 120
room, 18

safety, 35
sailing, 4
scale, 23, 26, 27, 29, 33, 34, 46, 48, 49, 51, 88, 95, 117
scandal, 106–108
school, 90
scope, 109
scrutiny, 41, 98, 100, 101, 103, 106–109
search, 39

section, 1, 5, 7, 9, 11, 13, 14, 16, 18, 23, 25, 27, 34, 36, 40, 41, 45, 49, 51, 57, 63, 65, 68, 71, 82, 87, 103, 105, 113, 117
sector, 65–68, 70–72
self, 1–7, 9–16, 29, 34, 42, 52, 63, 82, 90, 91, 98, 99, 102–105
sensationalism, 108
sense, 1, 7, 10, 12, 17, 20, 21, 23, 31, 49, 56, 60, 67, 82, 91, 93, 94, 101, 108, 119
separation, 107
series, 27, 58, 90
seriousness, 107
servant, 62
service, 41, 46, 112, 120
set, 31, 36, 40, 42, 47, 48, 51, 61, 62, 72, 80, 82, 98, 101, 105, 116, 120
setback, 26, 42
sex, 19, 21, 22, 28, 34, 46–48, 59, 60, 73, 80–83, 87–89, 93, 106, 111, 113, 114, 116, 119–121
sexuality, 4, 6, 10, 28, 88
shadow, 107
shame, 1, 5, 7, 32
shape, 6, 20, 29, 34, 74, 81, 90, 95, 109, 114, 115, 121
share, 16, 17, 23, 37, 41, 42, 46, 49, 51, 64, 89, 91, 101, 108
shift, 26, 50, 52, 60, 82, 88–90, 111, 115
show, 90
side, 4, 6, 10, 12, 14
sight, 59
significance, 32, 44, 45, 113, 116

Sigurlína, 10
Simon, 90
situation, 35, 55, 66
skepticism, 15, 40, 46, 56, 58, 69
skill, 49, 67
society, 2–8, 10–14, 16, 18, 20–23, 27–29, 32–36, 38, 39, 41, 42, 44, 45, 47–49, 51–53, 57, 59–61, 69, 70, 74, 77, 80–85, 87–95, 100, 102, 106, 109, 111–113, 115, 117–121
solace, 100, 107
solidarity, 17, 23, 114
solution, 8, 88
solving, 42
source, 45, 74, 88, 97, 100
space, 6, 17, 101, 103, 104
spark, 18, 101, 113
speaking, 52
spectacle, 18
spectrum, 8, 62
spending, 52, 70, 98, 102, 104
sphere, 3, 63
spirit, 100, 117
spotlight, 108
spouse, 107
spread, 73, 108
stability, 28, 56, 58, 59, 66, 68, 69
staff, 103
stage, 20, 28, 40, 55, 57, 62, 66, 68, 73, 74, 94, 114
stance, 63, 88
standing, 63, 66, 112
state, 55–57
status, 15, 18, 27, 42, 46, 82, 103, 113, 122
steadfastness, 107
step, 4, 36, 47, 63, 80, 81, 88, 103

stigma, 1, 10, 85, 88, 94
stigmatization, 117
storm, 107
story, 1, 5, 7, 21, 24, 29, 31, 33, 42, 47, 63, 90, 102, 112–114, 119, 121
storytelling, 11, 15, 16, 24, 25, 50, 51, 91
stranger, 6
strategy, 65, 108
street, 18
strength, 1, 4–7, 9, 11, 14, 24, 41, 42, 45, 46, 49, 58, 97, 100, 107, 108, 118, 119
stronghold, 106
struggle, 3, 5, 10, 31, 64, 81, 101
study, 67, 74
style, 43, 62, 117, 121
success, 32, 37, 40, 42, 46, 52, 71, 74, 86, 95, 100, 111, 114, 116, 120
suit, 20, 73, 88
suitability, 56
summary, 13, 38, 59, 106
support, 2, 4, 6, 9–14, 16–18, 21–28, 31–33, 35, 37, 40–47, 49, 50, 56, 58, 59, 61–65, 67, 69–73, 81, 91, 94, 95, 97, 100–107, 116
sustainability, 72
sway, 80
symbol, 29, 57, 62, 70, 73, 108, 114, 120
system, 21, 27, 28, 34, 36, 56, 57, 66, 67, 70, 94, 97, 101, 102, 104, 105, 107

table, 116, 120
tactic, 108

Index

tape, 71
task, 65, 67, 70
taxation, 27
team, 81, 99, 105
television, 89, 90, 92
telling, 11
tendency, 108
tension, 102
tenure, 56, 62, 68, 74, 83, 111, 113, 119
term, 57, 62, 66, 67, 69–72
test, 98
testament, 7, 9, 14, 63, 65, 68, 81, 113, 119
the North Atlantic, 93
thing, 4
thinking, 29, 42
threat, 69
time, 5, 12, 14, 24, 25, 32, 37, 40, 43, 52, 55–58, 60–62, 74, 98, 102, 104–106, 119, 121
today, 117
tolerance, 28
toll, 6, 58, 99, 100, 108, 109
tool, 23, 34, 49
tourism, 66, 68, 71, 72
town, 1, 17, 43, 65, 67, 69, 92
track, 58
trade, 72
trailblazer, 82, 111, 113, 114
training, 67, 84
transformation, 16, 60, 73, 87, 93, 112, 116
transgender, 17, 48
transparency, 32, 45, 56, 64, 65, 67, 69, 103, 107
treatment, 33, 81, 89
trial, 98
triumph, 11, 62

trust, 31–33, 37, 40, 43–46, 58, 64, 65, 67, 69, 70, 100, 103, 106, 107
truth, 107
turmoil, 58, 59, 61, 62, 66

understanding, 2–4, 10, 11, 15, 17, 22–25, 28, 29, 32, 34, 36, 39, 43, 44, 51, 52, 56, 60, 63, 65, 81–83, 88–92, 94, 97, 100, 111, 112, 115, 118, 119, 121
unemployment, 56, 57, 66–68
union, 7
uniqueness, 10
unity, 20, 44, 46, 60, 73, 91, 93
upheaval, 5
urgency, 55
use, 16, 24, 48, 117

vacuum, 58, 59
validation, 17, 19, 59, 82
value, 10
variety, 92
vehicle, 35
versatility, 33
victim, 28
victory, 62, 80, 83
view, 98
vigilance, 84
violence, 28
visibility, 24–26, 29, 74, 89, 112, 115, 116, 118, 121
vision, 13, 20, 21, 23, 33, 34, 37, 41, 49, 50, 52, 55, 58–64, 68, 69, 72, 92, 105
voice, 3, 13, 16, 20, 23, 25, 35, 36, 39, 41, 46, 49, 51, 52, 69
vote, 81

vulnerability, 71

wage, 27
warmth, 2
way, 1, 3–5, 7, 9, 12, 18, 20, 22, 23, 26, 27, 29, 31, 33, 37, 39, 40, 43, 45, 46, 51, 53, 56, 60, 61, 63, 64, 69, 82–84, 87, 88, 93, 95, 100, 112–117, 121
wealth, 27
weather, 40, 100, 106
weight, 2
welfare, 27, 56, 58, 59, 66, 67, 69
well, 6, 7, 20, 41, 52, 62, 63, 68, 87, 89, 99, 104, 108
wellbeing, 19
whirlwind, 1
whole, 36, 53, 117

willingness, 42, 64, 65, 90
woman, 7, 14, 39, 48
word, 44
work, 14, 21, 24, 26, 27, 36, 39, 41, 46, 49, 51, 52, 61, 74, 82, 88, 89, 91, 92, 108, 109, 111, 112, 116, 119, 121
workforce, 12, 67, 71
world, 1, 3, 7, 11, 13, 19, 20, 27, 29, 35, 39, 40, 45–47, 59, 60, 63, 73, 74, 80, 82, 84, 88, 90, 93, 94, 101, 105, 111, 113–119, 121
worth, 1, 82, 98, 100
writer, 99

youth, 17, 28

Ólafur, 10

Milton Keynes UK
Ingram Content Group UK Ltd.
UKHW020318021124
450424UK00013B/1324